UFO CRASH SECRETS

by James W. Moseley

Caption—A photo of the author taken in the late 1960s standing next to the famous late-night radio talk show host, Long John Nebel.

Cover art by Jim Dallmeier

INTRODUCTION

WEIRD HAPPENINGS AT WRIGHT PATTERSON

When a UFO crashed outside the town of Roswell, New Mexico in July, 1947, rumor spread that the wreckage—as well as the remains of several alien beings who had been onboard the ill-fated craft—was quickly gathered up by the military, put on the back of a flatbed truck and hauled away. Within hours—at the most several days—the ship and the badly-burned aliens—were flown to Wright-Patterson Air Force Base for scientific analysis and research purposes.

Speculation that a mysterious building known as "Hangar 18" might contain the remains of these small, gray-colored, extraterrestrials and their vehicle has remained constant over the years. Supposedly, there have been other crash landings in addition to the one at Roswell, and whatever was found—wreckage and bodies—ended up stored in this facility near Dayton, Ohio.

Such accounts have been fueled by the fact that the Air Force's various UFO projects (including Project Blue Book, its most famous) have been headquartered at this base. In addition, there have been many bizarre tales told by various retired military personnel who, while stationed at Wright-Patterson insist they "stumbled" upon the "truth" when they saw with their own eyes what they couldn't at first believe, and which they were later told to shut up about by their superior officers.

Furthermore, it remains a curious fact that even the likes of Senator Barry Goldwater has not been allowed inside this highly restricted area even though he is a retired Major in the Air Force and possesses a Top Secret security clearance. Goldwater, over the years, has written several letters to various researchers verifying this. Thus, it remains a puzzle why—if Hangar 18 doesn't contain something very unusual—he would not have been granted the right to inspect the inside of this facility.

Those who have followed UFOs will instantly recognize the name James W. Moseley, for Jim has a reputation in the field for being "older than dirt," in that he has been trying to track down these elusive disks as far back as the early 1950s. A veteran researcher who currently makes his home in Key West, Florida, Moseley is the former editor and publisher of **SAUCER NEWS** (a magazine that in its heyday had nearly 10,000 subscribers), and he once put on the largest indoor UFO convention of all time, attracting 15,000 to the three-day event held at New York's Hotel Commodore in 1967. Moseley—as those who know him can testify—is a no nonsense sort of guy when it comes to UFOs. Though he'll give just about anyone the benefit of the doubt, he's always questioning, probing, trying to get to the heart of the matter regardless of the outcome oo what repercussions it may have.

Way back in 1954, Jim tried to get onto Wright-Patterson Air Force Base and was turned away. "I happened to be passing through Dayton," Moseley recalls "and decided to telephone the base. I managed to get through to the officer then in charge of the UFO project. However, I was told that no one except accredited newsmen were allowed on the base, and that was the end of it!"

Over the years, Jim would drop in periodically at the Pentagon in Washington to interview whoever was in charge of releasing UFO information to the public. Several times he tried to get the okay to visit Wright-Patterson Air Force Base. Finally, on March 28, 1962 he was admitted to the facility—no cameras were to be permitted and he was asked not to name the exact building where he was taken.

"I had no opportunity to see any rooms other than the one in which my host, Col. Friend, worked. But in the halls were signs reading, approximately, 'This is a Security Area.' For the most part, Moseley's trip to the base was uneventful—certainly he was not shown the contents of Hangar 18. But he did learn something about the way UFO reports were handled.

"At Wright Field, all cases are accurately filed both according to date and location....Then, after Wright-Patterson's complete analysis has been done, approximately 2% of the cases are re-investigated personally either by Col. Friend or any of four other officers at his disposal, who are sent out from the base to the area, wherever it may be, that the sighting took place....In analyzing and solving UFO reports, Wright Field has at its disposal equipment which could not be duplicated by civilian researchers without the expenditure of many thousands of dollars—or perhaps millions. Col. Friend has, when necessary, the use of photographic, chemical and aeronautical laboratories. By simple phone calls, he can consult with aircraft project chiefs concerning experimental aircraft flights, or with personnel who have complete data about missile, satellite and balloon launchings."

While at the base, Jim says he only saw or heard one thing which seems pretty peculiar—if not downright mysterious. "There was a blackboard in Col. Friend's office with peculiar writing on it. This writing was peculiar because it obviously was not in our alphabet. I asked Friend about it, and he said (as nearly as I can recall) that it was a motto or saying, in ancient Syrian, which he had copied out of a book and which he had left up on the blackboard for the past week just to attract questions from visitors to his office. He told me that the motto was, but I unfortunately have forgotten it, as I did not write it down at the time. It was something nearly as commonplace as 'Never put off till tomorrow what you can do today.' But why put mottos in strange languages on the blackboard of an office devoted to serious intelligence work?"

Despite the fact that Jim might not have learned anything particularly earthshaking on his "official" visit to the base, it did not stop him from digging deeper and uncovering some potentially damaging evidence that the Air Force, the U.S. government, and the military, know a hell of a lot more about UFOs and aliens than they are letting any of us know about. This book should provide even further evidence that there is possibly something "not of Earth" inside Hangar 18!

The Publisher

Somewhere within the perimeter of Wright-Patterson Air Force Base is said to exist "Hangar 18," where crashed UFOs & Alien Bodies may still be stored!

Photos by James W. Moseley

11:45
THE FORBIDDEN PLANET
5

12:10
TWO MEN FROM VENUS
9

1:00
KIDNAPED BY SPACEMEN
22

1:45
SCOUT SHIP FROM VENUS
27

2:10
THE SAUCER BUG
34

2:35
THE AIR FORCE FILES
38

3:10
THE PUZZLED PROFESSORS
45

3:15
THE WRIGHT FIELD STORY
48

3:25
DR. D's STRANGE THEORY
53

3:30
THE TWELVE BEST SAUCERS
57

3:47
UFOs FROM ANTARCTICA
63

4:00
"THE SOLUTION TO THE FLYING SAUCER MYSTERY"
69

4:30
HUSH-UP!
74

11:45
THE FORBIDDEN PLANET

August, 1959. A hot night. The 24th floor. Microphones, and wires, and a room high above Times Square.

A blond man in a loud sports coat signaling, his long pointing finger reaching past those dials, into space, into the homes, into the automobiles, into the trucks.

Then a strange electronic beeping that filled the studio.

If there were Martians, this is probably their kind of music, I thought, as I listened to the squealing sounds change pitch and rise to a crescendo.

The cacaphony led into a beautiful melody. To a few people—buffs on remembering trivia, this music was, of course, David Rose's recording of *Theme From the Forbidden Planet.*

To those who twirled their radio dials at that hour, the electronic tonalities and the mystical, yet romantic theme, was now identified, however, with one single human voice.

"Good morning, neighbors. This is Long John." I tensed and squeezed tightly the object I held in my right hand, rolled up into a cylinder and crumpled. It was the latest issue of *Saucer News,* and it contained an article which would comprise the main agenda for discussion from midnight until 4:30 in the morning. It was the third time I had been on the Long John Show. As usual, I had stage fright.

I looked over the table at Gray Barker, who appeared amazingly calm though he had armed himself with a small mountain of newspaper clippings, copious notes, and several copies of books which he, the popular West Virginia publisher, had brought out about UFOs.

He would be on the hot seat tonight. I would charge, as I had printed in *Saucer News,* that

Barker had dressed up three men in strange black suits and hired them to frighten Al K. Bender into an abrupt silence.

Rabbi Y.N. Ibn Aharon (shortened to just "Yonah" for ease of reference), would delve into a strange, otherworldly book, titled *Oahspe,* sometimes termed a new Bible, its very title translated as "sky, earth and spirit."

He would charge that an anthropologist, named Dr. George Hunt Williamson, had set up a meeting by a man from outer space with Prof. George Adamski, and that somehow Barker had also been connected.

John Nebel wouldn't buy any of it—officially at least.

As Long John introduced the guest of the morning and the panel who would question him, I wondered if he only pretended to be skeptical about the array of offbeat personalities who regularly appeared before the microphones of his all-night show.

"Now, neighbors, I don't buy this," he would say, "but..."

And across the airways went the voices of people such as Howard Menger, who claimed to have· actually met with men from Venus. . .the Mystic Barber, who recieved telepathic beams from various planets. . .George Van Tassel, founder of the College of Universal Wisdom and designer of a rejuvenation machine. . .and, of course, Gray Barker, told fascinating tales of a Flatwoods Monster which had frightened seven of his neighbors out of reason on a bleak West Virginia hillside.

One of Barker's friends, Al K. Bender, had found out what the flying saucers actually were; others of his acquaintance had possessed pieces of the elusive discs, only to be silenced by threatening visitors, which some suggested to be none other than the space people themselves!

John believed *some* of it, I thought, else he wouldn't have so many offbeat guests on his show. Still the offbeat programming had been good radio boxoffice, and upped his ratings.

But regardless of how much he believed, or how much Gray Barker believed, I knew one thing: that I hardly believed one word of the charges I would level at the guest of the morning. Although I couldn't talk about some of the things which had happened to me, and would have to put up a highly skeptical facade throughout the show, I knew in my heart that I believed more than Long John and Gray Barker put together. But I would play the game. Probably that was what made me so nervous.

Barker relieved the tension by passing a note to me which simply said, "STENDAK!"

Long John Nebel caressed the microphone, placing his hands around its pedestal, and began the monologue to set the stage for the show. To the listeners John is presenting an absorbing synopsis of what has gone before; to a panel member in the studio, waiting to speak into his own microphone, it is fascinating.

John gets close to the microphone and seems to lose touch with those around him—the guests, the engineers, the producer and the people handing him commercials to read. Out of contact with the world, he speaks not to the microphone, for somehow in this brief period *he is the microphone*, the great mass of glowing tubes at the transmitter. Or to sum it up, at that moment *he is radio*.

Gray Barker, the author of a best-selling UFO book, *They Knew Too Much About Flying Saucers*, was up late and turning the radio dial when he heard John on one of his first radio shows. John was talking about flying saucers in a very skeptical manner. Barker angrily picked up the telephone and placed a long-distance call to the station. John had just installed one of the first so-called "beeper phones," whereby a telephone caller can speak over the air. He flipped a switch and Barker found hinself on the radio for the first time. John told him that if he wanted to put his money where his saucer was he could buy an airplane ticket, fly to New York and be on the show any night and talk as loudly and long as he wanted to. Barker took the challenge and walked into the studio the following week. Expecting to receive a kind of microphonic third degree, Barker, to his surprise, immediately found that John was letting him talk as much as he pleased—as long as

LONG JOHN NEBEL
Host of the famed all-night radio show on WNBC, New York. The author is especially indebted to Long John for allowing him to relate his experiences to the program's listeners, which number in the millions.

his flying saucer tales were interesting. So, taken by John's charm, he became a firm supporter of the fledgling show and shouted praises throughout the land, via his various publications.

I caught myself wondering why I was there in the studio, staying up all night, and discussing a subject which to the majority of Americans still was considered ridiculous. Ostensibly it was to get publicity for my magazine. Subscriptions and inquiries always poured in after an appearance on the show.

But I knew secretly that I wasn't here for subscriptions, or money, or for publicity. It went deeper than all that. And it all really started with *Krippine*.

When my mother died, early in my life, I had been thrown into the cold, outside world to fend for myself. Once in contact with that world of ordinary humanity, however, I found out for the first time that I was different. *For I was rich.*

Don't feel sorry for me. If you've never been rich, you should be. The wild tales of horror concerning the Rich Man, are mainly the inventions of the Rich to garner sympathy and toleration from the Poor.

At nineteen I began to Rebel Against Society.

I walked off the Princeton Campus in mid-semester and got hooked up with Ken Krippine.

That is how, in an incredible round-about way, I got on the "Saucer Kick."

Ken Krippine was an explorer of sorts who financed his jungle adventures by taking on safari a huge supply of Canadian Club and other products which later appeared in jungle-setting magazine advertisements. He also supported his anthropological researches by taking along young adventurers. Young enthusiastic rich adventurers paid through the nose for these "dangerous" jungle treks.

Ken was in his Peruvian period when I laid out a thousand dollars to accompany him on a South American trip to search for a lost city. I don't think he quite promised to lead me to the Lost Cave of the Inca Treasures, but I was interested in adventure, and my appraisal of Ken's oral prospectus led me to believe I would be safe from jungle rot, poisonous snakes and wild tribesmen.

One rewarding part of the safari was a side trip which Krippine didn't sponsor. While flying from inland to the coast of Peru, my interest in viewing the countryside below had diminished as we left the verdant jungles and the sameness of the desert passed below. I picked up a newspaper to pass the time away while the second-hand DC-3 vibrated and groaned. The president of Peru had given a huge number of pesos to assist a family afflicted with tuberculosis. Marilyn Monroe had made the Latin press. Land reform had been suggested by certain officials. In other words, the usual dull daily news of Peru.

I yawned and once again looked out of the small window—I blinked and looked again.

We seemed to be passing over a huge complex of modern roads, or a city. A closer look disclosed that what I was seeing was actually a series of strange geometrical markings on the Peruvian desert.

I nudged the local businessman sitting next to me, who awakened from his afternoon siesta long enough to take a cursory look. "Senor, those are nothing much. They are nothing but the Nasca Lines."

Once on the coast, the subject of the Nasca Lines continued to intrigue me. I stopped into a local museum, hoping to obtain an explanation.

The part-time curator, the local parish priest, searched through a pile of documents and came up with a small booklet, that, translated, was titled "Mystery On The Desert," and published in Peru by the British archeologist Maria Reiche.

"Only from an airplane," wrote Miss Reiche, "is it possible to appreciate the absolutely straight lines and borders of elongated surfaces, their great numbers, and the curious arrangement of stars, zigzags, and groups of parallels, and the strange network they form—as if traced on gigantic drawing boards...It is a strange fact that the ancient Indian designers probably never got a glimpse of the perfection of their own work, which can be seen well only from the air."

These lines, the curator Father Pacin explained to me, cover an area of more than 40 square miles, were made simply by overturning the reddish brown topsoil of the region to produce a pattern which from a distance looks something like white lines on a gigantic blackboard. Erosion is very slight in this region of Peru, and the lines and figures had survived the centuries with only a minimum of wear and tear.

In recent years treasure hunters had left their mark, particularly at the several points where the groups of lines intersect, their theory being that these points might have been the sites of temples or burial grounds.

So far, Father Pacin told me, nothing at all had been found in the diggings at the intersections.

I was intrigued by Miss Reiche's observations about the enormous amount of labor needed to produce the variety of large delineated surfaces and the wide lines.

"The absolutely straight lines and borders which sometimes cross considerable distances, cutting through valleys and passing over hills without ever swerving from their original direction, are a feat of engineering which must have been accomplished through the astoundingly keen eyesight of their designer... Stranger yet than the skill needed in tracing the lines and borders, is the technical accomplishment which was needed to solve the complicated problem of the transfer of the elaborate figures from models, which must have existed, to a scale at least a hundred times larger. It is hard to imagine how these ancient peoples with their limited knowledge could have projected these complicated patterns with such precision onto the desert." Miss Reiche goes on to say that even today, with modern skills and methods, the job of reproducing these figures would be fantastic.

I thanked Father Pacin and made a small contribution to the upkeep of the museum by placing a few pesos on one of the large antique stones at the entrance of the museum. I made a mental note to ask Krippine his opinion of the Nasca Lines; this might make a good subject for a magazine article or even a book if enough research could be done.

"Naw!" Krippine concluded after reflecting a few minutes while he concentrated on the cigar smoke curling over his head.

"Not fantastic enough."

Then he straightened from his relaxed position as he apparently had a new thought.

"Say, Kid"—that's what he always called me.

"Did you ever think that those lines can be seen only from the air? Yet they were made centuries ago, before we had aircraft. What if the people in that area were in contact with these flying saucers, which people claim to see, saucers that were around in these *early* days."

I had read the saucer reports and had been mildly interested. I liked to read science fiction books, and I somehow had connected the saucers with SF.

"Oh yes," he continued. "The flying saucers were probably contacting these early peoples of Peru, and the people regarded them as gods. They, probably with the help of these space people, created the ground markings as landmarks for these hokey Martians."

I could tell by his tone and facial expression that he did not believe a word he was saying.

I had seen a book Ken had been reading. It was the now classic and familiar *Behind the Flying Saucers*, by Frank Scully.

"Look (I remember his exact words), if you want to write a book which will get published easily, here's a good thing," and he handed me Scully's book. "But, Ken, I don't know anything about flying saucers."

"That's all for the better. You won't be prejudiced, so you probably could come up with a great book about them—with my help, guidance, *and my usual financial share, of course.*"

I gathered that Ken's many books had been largely farmed out in similar ways. Though remarkably colorful, adventurous and talented in many ways, Ken wasn't the type who would follow the discipline of bending over a typewriter for long sessions.

"When you get back home, head for Los Angeles. It's the center of the flying saucer cult. Get yourself plenty of wild stories, when with my help we'll come up with an expose type of book which will be worth a few grand in paperback. I'll even let you put your own name on it if you'll do the actual work and handle everything through me."

"But why," I asked, "an expose type book. Isn't there any truth to these flying saucer stories?"

"I doubt it. I think Frank got took." Again he referred to Scully's book which he picked from a table. "You never can tell," he added; "before I left New York, Holt told me thay had just sent Scully a royalty check for twenty thousand—that's pretty large change, considering the book racket as it is today."

Ken outlined a plan whereby I would do the research and come up with a rough manuscript. He would read it and farm it out to a hack for a finished draft. I would get my name on the book as author, but would sign a contract to give him half the royalties.

I could hardly contain my enthusiasm. Half the royalties of an intangible but somehow immensely promising project seemed to me astronomical. I would probably get on the "Tonight" and "Today" shows to promote the book. I would be autographing copies that crowds of admirers would push toward me.

I probably would be famous.

12:10
TWO MEN FROM VENUS

While packing for the trip to the green Ufological pastures of the West Coast to bait the "crackpots," a somewhat logical thought halted my impulsive rush.

In my haste to get on with the book project I had not realized that I knew practically nothing about the subject itself, nor did I have the first idea about whom to contact or interview after I arrived. I called up LA and had my hotel reservation set back a day, hoping this would give me some time for preparation.

As we talked about August C. Roberts and Dominick Lucchesi on the Long John Show, it seemed impossible that at one time I did not know this fantastic duo. Dom and Augie had figuratively pushed me off the diving board for my first plunge into the strange waters of Ufology.

I sat down in the middle of my living room, with my baggage all around me, for, strangely enough, it often seems that I do my best thinking when I am in disorganized situations. I had a little something to go on. In the back of my mind I remembered a New Jersey newspaper story about a local man who had witnessed and photographed a spectacular saucer. Though I had been only vaguely interested in the subject of flying saucers, I thought that I may have clipped out the item.

I suppose that psychologists would classify my youth as "a quiet reserved sort of kid." I had a habit of clipping out interesting stories and pasting them into scrapbooks—instead, I suppose, of the more acceptable social norm of going out and raising hell.

The only organization one could claim for these scrapbooks was that they were chronological. So, remembering that the story had appeared about a year back, I looked into the 1952 volumes.

Things began to ring a bell as I got into the August dates, but it was not until I thumbed back to June that the subconscious memory link was explained. The man who photographed the saucer was August C. Roberts, of Jersey City.

Roberts was on a skywatch tower, the story related, when he and James Leyden spotted the incredible thing over the New York skyline. Roberts told reporters it looked like a huge shiny coin, tilted with its edge toward them. It hovered briefly, then vanished in a burst of tremendous speed.

Augie grabbed Leyden's Brownie camera and snapped two shots. Unfortunately the shutter was set on "time," and he only got a blurred image on film; nevertheless the paper had run the two photos with a lengthy story.

The skywatcher's sighting had been accompanied with "a strange feeling, like nothing I ever felt before," and for no logical reason. Roberts felt certain that the object was an interplanetary spacecraft!

I decided Roberts might be the man who could give me some leads on saucer bugs. A check in the phone book disclosed no such person listed in Jersey City, so the next day I called his employer, mentioned in the story, found that Roberts was unmarried and boarded at his sister's house.

Once located by phone, however, he didn't sound like the crackpot I had expected. He said the paper had misquoted him, that he had no definite opinion as to what the object had been, and that he would gladly open his extensive UFO files, collected since this sighting, to me. He suggested that we meet that evening at the home of a gyroscope technician, also interested in saucers. Dominick C. Lucchesi likely could give me a number of West Coast sources of information, for he had corresponded with saucer buffs out there.

But Dominick was frightened, he added, because of an incident involving a friend of his who had got hushed up, as Augie put it, and he would have to check with Dom. A few minutes later he called back and said they would be glad to meet with me, provided they could tape record the entire conversation!

Although the condition was odd, I quickly assented. As I thought about it I felt the beginnings of my own paranoia, which I have since discovered runs quite universally through the field; meanwhile I was wondering just what value a tape recording of my conversation would be to them, and what the frightening experience he mentioned had been.

Once inside Dom's book lined apartment, I was plunged into a bizarre promenade of various UFO theories and bits of information, and was certain what I was learning there would make the supposed West Coast saucer mecca anticlimactic.

After Long John Nebel had finished setting the scene and I was called upon to talk, I referred to the *Saucer News* article by Lonzo Dove and commenced to assail Gray Barker.

Gray, I told John's listeners, had perpetrated a cruel hoax upon Albert K. Bender. He may have been one of the Men in Black himself! But, at the least, he had hired three men, possibly actors, possibly flying saucer enthusiasts of cynical attitudes, and they had visited Bender and scared the living saucers out of him. Barker had gone on the air knowing that it was just a radio show and that I didn't believe in the article, and he was all set, he promised, to make his rebuttal calmly.

But once on the air, the sincerity and belief which he finds difficult to admit to close friends, began to come across, as he angrily denounced the author who had quoted him out of context. John called a temporary halt to the program while producer, Dave Field, put a neck microphone on the angered West Virginian, who, forgetting he was on the air, persistently wandered off mike.

I still didn't know whether to believe Bender or not, though certainly Barker, who had written practically an entire book about the Bridgeport, Conn., saucerer, was sold on him. Once I had made my opening statement and Barker, Long John and the rest of the Panel had caught the controversial ball, my mind flashed back to my first meeting with Dom and Augie and my first encounter with the mystery of Al Bender and the three men in black suits.

August C. Roberts and Dominick C. Lucchesi

had belonged to a sort of correspondence club which collected information about flying saucers. Albert K. Bender, the head of the organization, had by accident come across some accurate information about the origin and purpose of the discs, and had been told to stop—possibly by the government, my hosts thought.

The odd thing, though, was the black suits the three men, who visited Bender, had worn. Whoever they were, they had confirmed the secret information Bender had come by, then had severely threatened him. He was so fightened by the visit that he became physically ill. He wouldn't tell Augie and Dom who the men were, what agency they were from, or, of course, the secret they had sworn him to keep.

Dom had conjectured as to what the Bridgeport man had found out, and hoped he hadn't done anything wrong by sending Bender his own engineering plans for an actual disc-shaped plane which would utilize jet power. Could that have been what the men were interested in? He doubted it. It had been his own idea, and he wasn't even sure it would work if it were actually built.

Dom and Augie were afraid they might also be visited and put under security regulations which would prevent their further research into the subject.

I thought they were overly anxious, though I was quite intrigued by the Bender mystery. After convincing them, though not entirely, that I was what I claimed to be—merely a prospective author—they opened up and soon had my head spinning with weird saucer data.

Besides giving me the names of many interesting personalities on the West Coast, they also freely gave local, and even interplanetary information! My notes from the session read in part:

(1) "Earth to tilt due to ice cap at South Pole and destroy civilization as it did 5,000 years ago. Saucers here to prevent this.

(2) "Lucchesi's friend in Pennsylvania had contact with female saucer occupant, was given strange black box which may be extremely dangerous. Box isolated in unpopulated area.

(3) "Saucers may come from inside the earth, where cave dwellers are alleged to pilot these craft.

(4) "Apposition of Mars and frequency of saucers.

(5) "Saucers historical. Get Charles Fort's book."

Dom got onto a chair and pulled a thick volume

down from a high shelf of a huge bookcase. It was the classic *Books of Charles Fort*, a compilation of four different books written by a man who had enjoyed bedeviling scientists with accounts of phenomena they could not explain. Aside from his tongue-in-cheek proof that the world was flat and that the Moon was only 37 miles away, Fort immediately impressed me with his years of gathering unexplained data.

Tucked away among this voluminous material are hundreds of accounts of unidentified flying objects antedating by years and centuries the relatively recent reports which began in earnest during 1947 and reached a peak in 1952.

No doubt Fort impressed other UFO writers, for his books have provided filler and mileage for so many of their books. I mention him in passing, partly to express the misgivings I was beginning to feel: Although the reports I had heard from Dom and Augie certainly bordered on the fantastic, here was a writer who had spent a great deal of his lifetime scientifically gathering such data. He quoted from learned magazines and other scholarly sources.

Perhaps not all of the flying saucer reports could be dismissed as crackpot.

As I steered my Ford onto the New Jersey Turnpike which would lead to myriads of roads finally connecting with the wild freeways of Los Angeles, I reflected on my good fortune in finding the saucer photo in my scrapbook, and its leading me to Dom and Augie. They had not only filled me in on the UFO field but had given me a number of suggested contacts in LA.

And as the turnpike unwound before me I could not foresee other lucky breaks. It was impossible to predict how my visit to a relative in a movie studio would lead to a near-encounter with a man from Venus! Or how I would meet one of the most fascinating human personalities in the strange world of UFO research: Manon Darlaine.

I cerainly won't embarrass my cousin by giving his identity here, for he's made quite a name for himself in a popular television series, and gained some stature as a solid Hollywood citizen of the type which film industry apologists often point to in a moment of civic pride. I doubt if he'd want it known that he has a relative who is a nut on saucers.

This was during his early, hard luck days, and he had just appeared in a number of ridiculous Class "D" movies. When I telephoned him to say hello, he suggested that I visit the movie set, where he

was working in a minor role, the next day. He would introduce me to some stars, and generally entertain me.

I found the making of motion pictures one of the most boring procedures I had ever watched. The crew was shooting one scene, that of a soldier torturing some French peasants, over and over, with delays between shots.

My cousin's agent dropped by early in the day, shortly after the gosh-awful Hollywood work day began at 7:00 a.m., to take him off the set for a meeting with a producer, and I was left to fend for myself. I wandered around the set until lunch time, wondering how I could make an exit without offending my host, when I happened to speak to a woman who turned out not only to be a gold mine of saucer information, but a dear friend as well.

Manon Darlaine was a free-lance consultant retained by many studios on set decoration, particularly in her specialty, French provincial design.

Sensing that I was bored, Manon took the trouble to talk with me, asked if there was anything she could show me or explain to me. I confessed my lack of interest in what was going on there and invited her to lunch at the studio commissary.

When I happened to explain my mission in L.A., her eyes lighted up, and to my surprise, I became the recipient of a torrent of information about the very things I was looking for.

"Maybe I can take you along when I meet Venutio!" she said. She was tremendously excited. A man from Venus had volunteered information about himself to *The Los Angeles Times*, she informed me, and she was hot after a personal interview with him. She also did some reporting for a French newspaper syndicate, and all her papers were yelling for space information.

Only after many years of friendship with Manon Darlaine would I discover the wide and varied background she had enjoyed before becoming a United States citizen. She had worked with the French Underground during World War I, and possessed what she termed "seven safes" full of information that would "shake" not only the U.N. and the UFO field, but Hollywood itself! I remember the difference given to Manon on the set by a famous but aging film queen, who happened to be visiting a young actor, her current *bon amour*. I gather that Manon was no person to be lightly reckoned with, either by the space people or Hollywood stars!

Somehow it seems, in retrospect, that the great

This photo of alleged flying saucer occupant, published originally in a German newspaper in the 1950's, has never been authenticated. The two men leading the "little man" were purported to be FBI agents.

12

characters one meets while investigating saucers are as gratifying as the stories they provide. In this respect I shall always warmly remember people such as George Adamski, Orfeo Angelucci, Gray Barker, George Van Tassel (to name only a few), and, of course, Manon Darlaine.

Though of advancing age, probably in her 80's, she preserved a vivaciousness, poise and kind of beauty seldom approximated by the young starlets who walked through their scenes at the studios where she worked. Rumor has it, and in Hollywood rumor is more important than fact, that she was once a great beauty who toppled two French governments.

It was through Manon that I became personally enmeshed in one of the strangest saucer cases I have ever been involved with—that of "Venutio," or "Mr. Wheeler," the man who came from Venus to find out if Venusians could mate with L.A. women and produce offspring. This in itself—a male who evidently favored paternity cases—was enough to send any reporter, Ufological or otherwise, panting toward a typewriter!

Somehow Manon had managed to work her way into the action when a *Times* reporter who wrote under the pen name of Mortimer Bane let it leak out that two not-too-strange-looking, but nevertheless odd, men had visited his cubicle and announced they were from Venus and wanted to sell their story.

I perked up my ears at once, for this was one of the things Krippine had told me to look for. I assumed that the reporter had sensed that flying saucers was a good subject for the moment, probably planned to write a book, and had cooked up the story.

I don't know if Manon had mentioned the Seven Safes to Bane, or whether or not he gave her the information willingly, but he had promised her a meeting with "Venutio" so that she could write a story for the French syndicate.

Manon made the appointment and the two of us invaded Bane's cramped quarters.

"I'm sure it's a hoax," he told us, "and that (he used curse words) is behind all this."

Then he told us how a year previous, this particular friend, a special effects man at one of the studios, had perpetrated a most remarkable hoax at his expense. An impeccably dressed Irishman had introduced himself, and in a remarkably matter-of-fact manner informed Bane he had won $10,000 on the Irish Sweepstakes, then had gravely handed him a cashier's check in that amount. That Bane had not bought a ticket,

or even been approached, made no matter; in fact it had served to increase the believability when the man told him how a maiden aunt in Old Erin had purchased it in his name. Bane fell for this, though he had been hoaxed more than once before—with the same man begind it all. Of course, the check proved to be a complete fabrication, a product of the studio printing department which produced various documents for on-camera closeups. Since that department had just forged the Magna Carta, for a historical film, Bane felt some small comfort in being taken in by experts. Even better than this one was the pitiful lady with the infant, which situation I won't go into here; nevertheless Bane admitted he had fallen for that one.

"But this time I have his number," he announced. "I have a laboratory analyzing how he did THIS."

Bane pulled out a photograph of a piece of metal which appeared to be an engraving plate.

I could sense that Bane genuinely liked Manon Darlaine—perhaps she affected other people that way too—so it seemed that in deference to her he repeated some of the story to me.

"Five weeks ago, this kook comes in here with another character. The one sits down there (he pointed to a chair) and the other just stands here glaring at me and finally says, 'I'm Mr. Wheeler, and I have come from Venus.'

" 'Sure,' I say; 'tell me all about it!' And he DOES. He's parked his space ship on the desert. You people probably don't know this, but on Venus, you see, due to the carbon dioxide in the atmosphere and all that strange jazz, it's pretty hot and dry. Just like the desert around here. So these kooks pick L.A. for it's more like their own planet.

"They want to sell me this story, like so many other nuts that sift in here through the woodwork, and of course I've got no budget, even though Jesus Christ himself would show up.

"Before I could throw him and this other weirdo out of here, Venutio—this Wheeler guy—says he can show me he's actually from way out from the fifth planet—or whichever planet it is. He takes his thumbnail and with proper ceremony puts a deep scratch in the trim of the desk—here, look!"

There was a deep gash in the desk trim, but it didn't prove anything to me—though Madame Darlaine, sensing a good story, took copious notes.

"I figure the guy has a sharp piece of metal from the studio machine shop in his fist, and I go along with it, not wanting at that stage of the game to let on that I was hip."

I got the impression that Bane was a man who

protested too much: He had found Venutio's story too credible for his own comfort, and was this blustery, though good-natured manner he employed in relating the account a part of CONVINCING HIMSELF it WAS a hoax?

This was more apparent as he continued the narrative. After he put the two strange men off by promising to speak to his editor about buying their story, they left, promising to return later.

One of them, Venutio, did return the following day, but had changed his mind about selling the story. He had decided he didn't want publicity about his work on Earth, but did need money to buy food. He asked Bane to secure a job for him.

"Whether or not it was a gag, I decided to keep going along," Bane told us. "So I called Hatch Graham—he's the deputy public defender—and told him, 'Hatch, I've got a man for you. He's from the planet Venus, but he needs a job and you were just asking me for a leg man last week.'

"Sure, send him over!' Hatch has a really princely sense of humor. As to Venutio's fine record helping him track down witnesses, you'll have to talk with Hatch. He hired Venutio out of the fund he uses for occasional investigators and informers."

Bane then added a few more details about Venutio: He and the other man did not appear abnormal, just a bit strange. Their eyes, he thought, were wider apart than an average fellow's, and they had small ears, but not abnormally small. They were ruddy complexioned and their nostrils seemed a bit wide. "Just weird enough to make you a trifle uneasy, though you couldn't quite pin it down. My pal when he hired these extras must have really looked over a lot of people. He certainly didn't just pick them off the street. They didn't talk like bums; in fact their english was impeccable, except for an occasional misuse of a word. They were probably faking these misused words to go with their story of learning English back on their planet, listening to radio programs emanating from Earth."

"What about the interview with them? Is it set up yet?" Manon inquired.

Bane's gruff tone changed and a look of genuine disappointment came over his face.

"You'll think I'm giving you the business. But you're a real nice girl, and this is the gospel. Venutio worked a few days for Hatch and disappeared. Neither of us has seen hide nor hair of him since. He's gone back to Venus—or he's got enough money to bum it to some other town."

He picked up the phone and arranged for us to interview public defender Graham.

Hatch Graham was much more serious about Venutio than Mortimer Bane had been.

"I only wish he hadn't vanished," he told us. He then related how Venutio had quickly found slippery witnesses and other sources of information important to the cases of poor clients his office was defending.

"Venutio claimed he found them in routine ways, such as looking up job records and the like—but he found people whom other investigators had failed to locate. It was almost as if he had occult powers."

"I kidded Bane that he was responsible for the disappearance," Hatch told us, and he smiled broadly. "I guess after talking to him you've found out how much this spaceman idea— whether or not it is a hoax—has bugged him. If somebody is pulling his leg, they really have him going!"

"Bane kept after me constantly the moment I hired Venutio. Did I believe it? Could we prove it was a hoax? I told him that to me it didn't matter as long as he was doing such an excellent job. I'm afraid I did pull his leg, myself. I was a trifle annoyed with his constant concern, so I made up a little thing or two about the remarkable accomplishments of Venutio the Venusian. But I really didn't have to exaggerate; this man was uncanny!

"Finally Bane came up with a really wild idea. I should have the police detain Venutio on suspicion, have him fingerprinted, and, most important, strip him down to see if certain details about his body, given to Bane by the spacemen, checked out.

"I didn't want to do this. Venutio, whether from Venus or Ventura, seemed to be an all-right guy, despite this queer line. I couldn't conscientiously have him held for interrogation. I put Bane off by telling him that Venutio probably had telepathic powers and seemed to know things that were going on behind his back. 'If you aren't careful,' I told Bane, 'he'll pick up your thoughts and go back to Venus, or some other city on Earth. Don't ask me to lose a good leg man!'

"I believe Bane took me seriously. He seemed satisfied and hung up. He didn't get a chance to bug me any more, for Venutio never showed up again.

"In fact," he added, "Now I almost believe my own story."

The telephone interrupted Graham.

He covered the mouthpiece after listening a minute or two, definitely exhibiting surprise. Then a smile played over his face and I could tell from certain references that he was talking to Bane.

"Well, Venutio has him going again," he told us. "You better get over there right away. I think he really has something for you."

Manon and I hurried back to the TIMES office.

"You know what that creep friend of mine has done!"

(Bane was still referring to the special effects man as he stood staring at a paper in his hand.)

"He's bought off this whole damned laboratory!"

His hand shook visibly as he handed us the document.

During Venutio's second visit to Bane's office the reporter had asked him to repeat the feat of scratching surfaces with his fingernail, only that time he offered him a steel engraving plate such as is used in special kinds of printing. Venutio had, with one stroke of his amazing thumbnail, made quite a dent in it.

I have recently read a magazine article which purports to cover the Venutio story accurately.

The account reports on an analysis by the Smith-Emery Company, a highly-reliable and respected testing laboratory. In the article the report states that metallic deposits, foreign to the usual composition of such a steel engraving plate, had been present: calcium, lead, strontium, cobalt, etc.

But the lab report Bane offered to us did not say this.

I DID NOT MAKE AN EXACT TRANSCRIPT OF BANE'S LAB REPORT, BUT IT VERY SIMPLY STATED THAT THE LABORATORY HAD DUPLICATED THE SCRATCH ON THE SAME PIECE OF METAL, AND THAT THE LOAD REQUIRED TO MAKE THE INDENTION AMOUNTED TO 1700 POUNDS!

(In next issue: Another condensed chapter of Mr. Moseley's book, titled "The Missing Film". Learn how the confiscation of film footage of a flying saucer exposed the identity of the Silence Group and bankrupted a motion picture producer. These revelations never made public by Moseley prior to this time.)

12:45
THE MISSING FILM

Barker was winning the debate, and Long John had temporarily withdrawn from the discussion, sitting back from the microphone, enjoying our defeat. John usually takes the part of an underdog, and he was getting a visible kick out of seeing Barker defend himself so capably.

The *Saucer News* article, accusing him of being one of the "Three Men In Black," seemed logical to me when I published it, but now it didn't seem to hold water as Barker countered it, point by point.

About the only avenue of attack that Yonah and I saw open was to insist that Barker was making huge profits on the flying saucer books he published and sold. While indeed such a profit-making situation is acceptable to society nowadays, somehow it seemed that if you accuse a saucerbook author of making money, you make him look bad.

This put Barker on the defensive. For a while it seemed the panel might be winning, but I still remember wishing that I was back in Los Angeles, working on my first saucer investigation, hearing for the first time the Venutio story and other incredible narratives.

My mind flashed back to the information Manon Darlaine had given me, along with her advice not to telephone a certain producer before I walked in on him at his office. He had made a flying saucer film with allegedly authentic footage of an actual space ship, which had been filmed in Alaska, according to her informant.

This producer shall be nameless here, for since my interview with him he happened to "hit" with a teenage picture cycle that made a million bucks. He has now been graduated to major film production.

I had always pictured a Hollywood film producer's office as a luxurious affair, in a plush section of town, with deep carpets and sexy receptionists. When I walked into the sleazy hotel and rode the ancient elevator up 15 flights and knocked on a door, I was entering the world of the film producer of the late 40's. It was the world of the quickie independent film production, which managed to survive in the movie-hungry market occasioned by the burgeoning of drive-in theatres.

Not realizing the money potential to be derived from renting their best films to the outdoor theatres, the major producers had hesitated to leave their "hardtopped" indoor theatre markets. Meanwhile the "passion pits", as the pious termed the drive-ins in those days, had put a new kind of producer into business: a fellow familiar with movie production who could scrape together a hundred thousand dollars to make a cheap, sensational type of film. Once the production was finished, processing laboratories would usually put up money for advertising and supply the film prints in return for a lucrative first mortgage on the picture. If the film did not do well in drive-in theatres, there was always the hungry infant, television, which at that time was still unable to obtain much major film footage and would buy practically anything.

I was about to interview such a mortgagee.

A bespectacled young man, with suspicion evident on his face, opened the door marked (I use a pseudonym) Stellar Productions. With the door open just enough to see through the crack, and not enough for a more aggressive caller to get his foot into, he inquired about my business.

It took a couple of minutes to convince the man that I was neither a process server nor a creditor. He admitted me after he was convinced that I was only a prospective writer wanting to know about the flying saucer film the company had shot.

He said that the producer (I'll call him Frank Miller) was due in any moment, and no doubt would be willing to talk with me. He offered me some trade papers to read, but I found these dull and, instead, pulled out some notes I had made while visiting the head of the Civilian Saucer Investigation, one of the earliest UFO investigative groups in the Nation.

In May of 1951, three technically trained men, Ed Sullivan, Werner Eichler and Victor Black, experienced a rather routine saucer sighting in the L.A. area, which, because of the background of the sighters, was given wide publicity—eventually appearing in *Life* magazine. As a result of the publicity, Sullivan decided to start a saucer investigation group, and invited the public to send in their sightings for analysis. The group grew to a dozen or so active members, and even attracted as

an honorary member Dr. Walter Riedel, one of the country's leading rocket experts. Largely through the *Life* publicity, Sullivan and his co-workers received and analyzed more than a thousand sightings, hoping to find hidden within this mass of data some elements of consistency that would eventually tell them what saucers looked like, how and why they behaved as they did. Unlike most researchers, these men began with no preconceived notions. Perhaps that was why they failed to arrive at any definite conclusions beyond similarities of size, shape and performance.

Sullivan's group found that each sighting seemed to represent a law unto itself in regard to details, and finally they realized that by no amount of study could they hope to fit all genuine sightings into one or more specific category. In other words, they failed to solve the mystery, though it had gradually become apparent to the investigators that

Although myriads of still pictures of UFOs have been taken, a relatively few motion pictures have been reported. Perhaps one of the most authenticated movies is represented above in the single-frame blowup inset. Major Colman VonKeviczky, of the American Institute of Aeronautics and Astronautics, and currently at the United Nations, New York, doing photographic technology, is seen here holding a series of blowups from the film. The movie was taken by Ellis E. Matthews, of Alberton, South Australia.

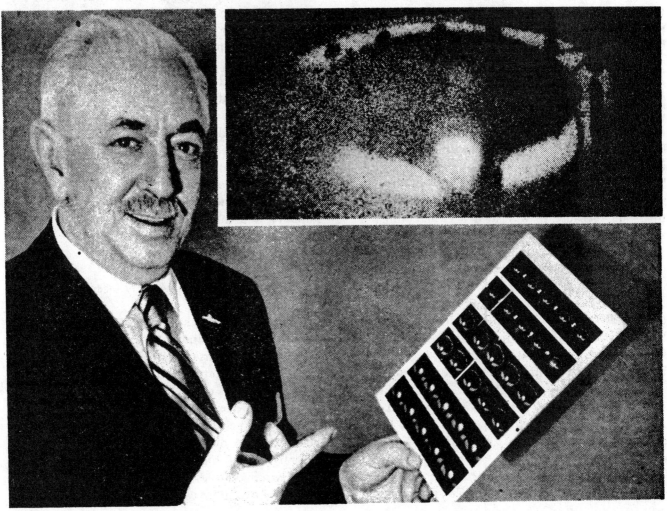

craft, probably from another planet, were responsible for the hard core or unexplained, sightings.

"We're not "hushed up' " Sullivan assured me, "so don't help to spread this rumor that is going around. We just found we were not equipped to solve the mystery, with our limited facilities of equipment, money and time, and we gave up."

I removed the group's last publication, which Sullivan had given me, from my portfolio.

"Then you run into this sort of thing," Sullivan told me, pointing to a report in the publication headed '1949 Sighting—One of the Most Interesting Reports Received by CSI.'

The writer is a college graduate who has had several years graduate study as well. For five or six years I have been a cattle breeder on a farm a couple of miles from G. An article in *Life* magazine, which I read last week, has brought to mind again an experience which took place in 1949. I have debated with myself for some time as to writing about it. At the time it happened I mentioned it to my wife, and to my wife alone; I had not then, nor do I have any desire to be considered now an ass, so please do not publicize my name. However, on the chance that this information may be of use to you, here is what happened:

I had run an expectant cow into the barn lot for delivery, since she has always had trouble delivering without aid. That night, a clear, rather chilly fall evening, I had stayed up past one a.m., reading, until time to go make a check on her before retiring. Our house faces south and the barn is to the north and some distance away from the house. With a bucket of warm water, some soap and twine, I left the house and stopped to look at the stars, because it was such a clear evening, I suppose.

To the south, in the form of an equilateral triangle, I noted three lighted bodies which I knew in an instant were not stars. For a moment I thought them to be airplanes, but then they moved too rapidly for even jet planes. Suddenly one (the leading one) peeled off from the formation and seemed to be coming directly at me. I was frankly terrified. I threw myself onto the ground and remember thinking what a poor place to be if struck. I guess I was praying and shaking at the same time. Suddenly, I had a feeling that I had nothing to fear, and I guess my curiosity was very great so I rolled over.

There it was, a little to my left (east) seemingly stationary. It was a few hundred feet off the

ground (my guess). I would also guess that it was between 300 and 400 feet in diameter. There appeared to be windows which seemed about twice as high as they were wide. These windows were evenly placed and were on the edge, where the over and the under curved surfaces came together. I noted that the other two had moved north, but had become stationary. This close one did not revolve. However, the longer I looked at it, the more I had a feeling of undulation. The thickness, I would guess to be a minimum of 75 feet and a maximum of 100 feet. It was absolutely without sound, but I had a very deep feeling that it embodied terrific energy.

The light coming from the windows, I would describe as being a blue-white, much as the color of a welding flame. Then I guess it was (after my feeling of undulation) that I became aware of (this is very hard to describe) a very, very powerful vibratory force. *Everything*, myself included, seemed to respond to this vibratory force. (That's the best way I can describe it). One such thought was that with the aid of this force, gravity meant nothing. Most of the rest of my ideas, then, were even more asinine. I don't know how long I lay there, wet from the spilled bucket, but peculiarly not at all afraid. Just as inexplicably, the thing took off with amazing speed to the north, and the vibratory feelings seemed to slacken and disappear. It took its lead position in the triangle, and all three zoomed off at the same rate of terrific speed. In regard to the light—after the thing left I was aware that I had a reddish glow before my eyes, as though I had been staring at a light bulb. Had the light been as in welding, I feel that the length of time I looked would have ruined my eyes.

It left me with an overpowering feeling of humility and insignificance. I sincerely hope this above will be of use to you.

S.E.

(This report was followed by a second letter six weeks later):

I received your acknowledgement to my earlier letter and was reminded of a plea which I heard when I sent the first letter off to you. I had taken the draft of my letter to G, a close personal friend, for his criticism of my attempt to recount a very personal experience to strangers. My friend insisted that I take the draft to Dr. B in that city. Dr. B is an advisor to the Atomic Energy Commission in Bio-physics and bio-chemistry and served with the U.S. government as a scientific consultant. He is also a representative for the People's Division of the United Nations. He read the draft through carefully, and when I asked him whether people would think it asinine to mention the impact of thought I was subjected to he smiled and said no, that it had long been recognized that sudden and great exposure to gamma rays had an effect such as I described. He urged me to tell all that I could.

First of all, the thing represented energy—powerful and elemental, but still *controlled*. There was nothing haphazard about it, whatever. The perfect proportion of the equilateral triangle in which the three moved, the regular spacing of the windows, the graceful and beautiful proportions of the thing itself, as well as the undulating, vibrational pattern I felt all pointed to wonderful thought—coupled with careful planning and execution.

The length of time which I spent on the ground could not have been long, but I honestly do not know how long I was there. I felt a desire growing to join myself to the thing. It was somewhat like hypnosis from what I have observed—although I have never been a successful subject for hypnosis. It seemed to have a much greater power than gravity. I had an impression that gravity was a cold magnetic action and that it was inferior in power to the hot magnetic action of the thing.

When I went to the barn, which has its opening on the east, I was startled to see my cow. An Angus, like the rest, she had two marked characteristics. First, she was definitely antisocial as far as humans were concerned, and second, she had never had a calf without aid. When I got to the barn I was dreading, after the experience I had been through, roping her and helping her calve. She was standing facing the entryway, with her hide shaking all over like a horse trying to shake off a swarm of flies. But she was not afraid. Her eyes showed no white whatsoever. She would let me touch her anywhere, and when I examined her I knew I did not need to go back for more water. She was back, in appearance, to a point weeks from calving. I turned her out and, as I recall, she had her calf unaided the next day.

Many of the mental impressions which I received were new to me. At least I don't recall ever having come across them before. However, they charged my mental battery, so to speak, so that I got into encyclopedias and other books, and found that all had been expressed before. In every case, which I can recall, the seemingly simple truths had been called to peoples' attention long ago. One result—after many years away from it—I returned to church when the full impact of realization finally struck me. It took two years and has changed a cocky guy into a very humble person.

I do not feel in any way that I deserve any credit for this experience. I stumbled into it both figuratively and literally. I again renew my request for anonymity.

S.E.

A key turning in the door of the cheaply furnished offece awakened me from my perusal of the relatively dull magazines. In walked a handsome man in his 30's with circles under his eyes and a worried look on his face.

"I'm Frank Miller," he said, offering his hand. His assistant filled him in on my mission.

"There's very little to it, except the Air Force ruined me," Miller told me ruefully. He flopped down in a chair and offered me a cigarette from the battered pack.

I began to like this man immediately, and I am extremely glad he has done well since our meeting. I recently ran into him on a plane and found he had lost none of his wit and down-to-earth manner. It is difficult to believe that he was giving me a leg-pull back in 1953.

"It all began when I engaged a friend of mine to make some sixteen millimeter film for me in Alaska. This chap bums it all over the world, picking up jobs here and there, including film assignments when he can. I was doing pre-production work on a science fiction film about a prehistoric monster which comes alive due to atomic bomb experiments. It is first seen in Alaska, then heads south for L.A.—and the whole bit. There is no good film clip library on Alaska and I needed some shots of the coastal region which we could use as background. If you shoot sixteen millimeter color film you can blow it up to theatre-size film pretty easily, without much distortion.

"Well, Skippy shot a couple hundred feet of film and was ready to send me the batch when he decided to make part of it over due to better weather. While getting a shot of the surf, this character notices a bright flash in the viewfinder and looks up.

"There, hovering a few hundred feet above him is a real weird flying saucer. Jerry, dig that original letter out of the files, and I'll even let him copy it if he wants to."

"I think you may have the most sensational sequence of film ever released by a Hollywood studio," the letter to Miller read, "and that you won't have to use any special effects after all. Now, I'm no scriptwriter or producer, but I think I have something for you and if you change the plot of your picture you can announce that you have actual photographs of a flying saucer in your picture.

"I'm air mailing the film directly to the lab you specified and you should get it from them without delay.

"Here's essentially what I saw and it should come out good on the film. When I looked up I saw an object like two dinner plates stuck together. On top of this was a dome with round windows or portholes. The object was a bright silver in color, with a greenish glow coming from underneath. As I watched and shot my film, I became aware of a high-pitched tone which made me rather uncomfortable. Then this flying saucer, if that's what it was, began to move, in a strange kind of gyration. It seemed to sway back and forth, describing a wide arc, just as if it were on an object suspended on some giant cable from the sky. As this swaying motion became faster, it suddenly shot upward at about a 75-degree angle to the southwest, the greenish glow changing to a bright yellow, then a deep red. There was a kind of 'shooshing' sound as it did this, but both the sound and the machine vanished within an incredible second or so."

As soon as he received the letter Miller immediately had had a quick rewrite done on most of the script. He changed it from the atomic monster theme to that of a flying saucer appearing and warning the public to stop nuclear testing, following somewhat the successful major studio film, The Day the Earth Stood Still.

He made the mistake, however, of sending out blurbs to all the columnists and to the trade press, announcing that his film would be the first to contain actual close-up movies of a genuine flying saucer.

This led to his undoing.

"An Air Force major in a natty uniform showed up," he told me, "and said he would like to know more about the film. Get me right, he didn't at any time discourage me from finishing studio shooting of the film, releasing it, or anything

"At the time, in fact, he seemed to be quite a decent chap. We had both been in the Pacific, and had seen action on the same island. But I had been an enlisted man and he had served as an officer throughout the war, so we had never talked to each other before. We went out to a bar and had a few drinks while he discussed the general flying saucer situation.

"He told me that many saucer sightings were dreamed up by crackpots and that many of the cases involved misinterpretation of various natural phenomena. The Air Force was greatly concerned about the reports, however, and actually had a special division set up to investigate many of the sightings.

" 'That, of course is the official Air Force policy line on the situation,' the major said.

"I asked him what he personally thought of them, and he said that although he was probably too much of a science fiction buff to be objective. he personally believed there was something to it and that it could be boiled down very simply—we were being observed by an advanced civilization from Mars!

"The Air Force, he told me, wanted to examine our film for authenticity. I told him I wanted no part of it, since frankly, if it were a fake or some sort of natural phenomena, I certainly didn't want this to get out and ruin our publicity. I had already made costly alterations to our shooting schedule.

"He assured me that the results would be kept in strict confidence, and noted that his superiors had anticipated just such a reaction from me. If the film we released caused a great deal of controversy they would wait a respectable length of time until it got through the key money playdates before announcing they had analyzed it. Regardless of how good the film was, it was the policy of the Air Force to attempt to explain all photos and sightings, the major added.

" 'Gee thanks!' I told him, 'but I still don't buy that. Are you demanding the film or just asking a favor?' I asked him.

" 'I wish I had the authority to do so, but I don't,' the major told me.

"Then he began to fill me in."

Miller said the major had described the Air Force's role in flying saucer investigation as a great dilemma. They had gotten into it because their job was to keep the nation secure from enemy aircraft attack. Any unidenified flying object suggested the possibility of enemy aircraft penetration. Suddenly the whole impact of the possibility of superior interplanetary civilizations had hit them, and they found themselves holding a much bigger bag than they anticipated.

The year 1952 had brought a big UFO scare. Flying saucers were seen everywhere across the Nation. Many were reported as landing. A monster scare gripped West Virginia.

"Whether it was just hallucinations or something real, there was the possibility of real panic if the Air Force had another 1952. They were trying to dig into all the cases and explain the ones they could honestly solve and to gather evidence which might provide the key to the solution of the mystery."

Miller hadn't believed in saucers from space, feeling they were some sort of secret military craft, but the major's appeal partly changed his mind. If it were one of our own craft his photographer had filmed, why would the Air Force be so anxious to examine the footage? So he put in a call to the lab, releasing the three rolls of film for a local Air Force officer to pick up, with the promise that they would immediately return the two rolls of background film, make a quick duplicate of the saucer footage on the third roll and forward the original to the studio where he was renting space and equipment for the movie.

"Three weeks passed and no film," Miller continued, so I called the major. He expressed surprise and promised quick action."

"He got quick action all right and I got a screwing. Skippy vows he sent about 25 feet of exposed film of the 100 on the saucer roll to the lab. I got back the two background footage rolls intact, but only about 15 feet of the other film, by registered mail within a week.

"I brought my two writers down to the apartment and ran the film off for them. It was the first time I had seen it, since the bulb in my projector had burned out and I had to look around the stores for the special kind it took. When I turned up the lights I must have looked like a fool; at least I cerainly felt like one.

" 'How do you write anything around that?' Bill, one of the two, observed, and he was correct. The movie showed a small speck in the sky which moved around slowly for about 30 seconds. What's more it wasn't even over the water, it clearly was a desert scene, though there wasn't a horizon reference. If you've caught the picture you'll know what I mean."

Miller trusted the free-lance photographer implicitly and was certain he had told the truth. He was a cinematographer of at least 25 years of experience. A telephone conversation with him, when he finally could be located, further confirmed Miller's suspicion that a substitute film had been foisted upon him.

Miller was in a real bind, for the "saucer film" really showed nothing that would convince anybody. The picture, already oriented around the sequence, had been completed, using the substitute saucer, but caused no stir and little patronage at the boxoffice. In fact it had received only a couple of hundred bookings, and these in second feature slot at minimum rentals. The corporation formed for the movie had taken bankruptcy and Miller was now desperately trying to get back on his feet.

I am happy to observe that Miller has since risen above this sort of producing, has garnered a couple of minor Academy Awards, and is no longer on the lookout for process servers.

1:00
KIDNAPED BY SPACEMEN

The advent of somehting which is pleasant, or something which is sad or, more often, with Ufologists, something tremendously exciting,—usually starts with the ringing of a telephone.

So it was on the Long John Show—and so it was in L.A.

Only John's phone doesn't ring. It either lights up or somebody motions from the control room to pick it up. As we continued the discussion John entered into his own private, but visibly heated, discussion with some unknown party on the other end.

Listening to the tape of this particular show and remembering what I could reconstruct from the audio reminders, I really think that whatever troubles beset the Long John Show that night started with John picking up the telephone.

If John ever retires, which I sincerely hope he will never do, though he live to be a hundred, I'll probably ask him what happened, if I'm around to do so. Meanwhile I'm sure he doesn't want to discuss it. But something strange was afoot that night, something that might help us all explain a lot that we don't know about official suppression of saucer information.

In L.A., the telephone had also rung, and I had it in my hand before I realized I had been awakened at 2:00 in the morning.

It was Manon Darlaine, and her voice was shaking.

"Jim!" she said, "I should have let you in on this when I gave you the lead on the confiscated film. I promised to keep this quiet, but I think you should know about this. Anyhow, the papers are swarming all over the story. It's no longer a secret."

I fumbled first for the light and then for my cigarettes.

"What! Manon! What's up?"

"A couple of men have been kidnaped by a flying saucer!" Then she gave me some details.

Two nights previous Karl Hunrath had telephoned her at about midnight. He and Jack Wilkinson were ready to keep an unusual rendezvous, and invited her to come along. They were on their way to meet a flying saucer crew and take a ride in their craft!

Although I gathered that since she was still evidently a part of the terrestrial scene, she had declined the invitation, I could detect a note of real excitement, fear and belief in her voice.

"I've just had a call from Mrs. Wilkinson," she continued. "Yesterday Hunrath and Wilkinson just walked off their jobs and rented a plane at the Gardena County Airport—that's near L.A. They didn't file any flight plans and they have completely desappeared!"

Maybe Manon was being overly dramatic as she first started to fix my breakfast in her studio apartment, went into an adjoining room and brought out a strongbox which she opened with a key tied around her neck. Inside were several file folders. She withdrew one and told me to digest it as thoroughly as possible, for she couldn't let the material out of her sight.

I have just dug the elaborate notes I made that morning from my research files, in order to put together the strange background of this duo of Hunrath and Wilkinson.

Karl Hunrath and His Associates was the title of the file folder, written on the tab with the elaborate calligraphy which she evidently reserved for important cases.

She apparently sensed some importance about

Wife Fears Hubby in Flying Saucer Kidnap

BY CHARLES RIDGWAY, Mirror Staff Reporter

Two missing electricians may have been kidnaped by interplanetary invaders in a flying saucer, fears Mrs. Wilbur J. Wilkinson of 1933½ LeMoyne Ave., wife of one of the missing men.

The two flying saucer fans, Wilkinson and Karl Hunrath of 2315 S Flower St., took off in a rented airplane from Gardena Airport last Wednesday with a three-hour gas supply.

Despite a widespread search, no trace of the plane or its occupants has been seen.

Wilkinson's wife told The Mirror today that Hunrath was an avid believer in flying saucers. He and Wilkinson believed the end of the earth was nearing, and that strange little men from the planet "Maser" were ready to invade.

Hunt Saucer

Hunrath claimed to know the whereabouts of a flying saucer recently landed. Wilkinson's den, in their rented hillside home, is lined with flying saucer pictures, weird signs and formulas, which his wife says were supposed to be the new interplanetary language.

"Of course, I don't quite go for all the flying saucer talk, but Karl had convinced Wilbur they actually existed," Mrs. Wilkinson related.

"He had tape recordings of conversations with men from other planets who landed here in saucers."

She also pointed to messages tacked on Wilkinson's walls, supposedly received by radio from the interplanetary visitors. One was from a "Prince Reggs of the planet Maser."

The Wilkinsons, who have three children, Patricia, 12; Judith, 5, and John, 2, moved here from Racine, Wis., June 28. Wilbur is employed by Hoffman Radio Corp., where he was recently promoted to be in charge of the inspection department, Mrs. Wilkinson said.

The 38-year-old electrician has a den full of electronic equipment, radios and tape recorders.

"He was planning to go into the recording business," his tearful wife told The Mirror.

"He really didn't seem too interested in flying saucers except when Karl Hunrath came around. Karl was the one who talked us into coming to California because he said he could actually show a flying saucer to Wilbur."

Deputy sheriffs took a dim view of the "saucer kidnaping."

They warned Mrs. Wilkinson the two missing men might be in for a prison term if it is shown they "stole" the plane.

Mrs. Wilkinson admitted having an argument with her husband the night before he disappeared, but insisted it had nothing to do with him leaving. "I just can't help but think flying saucers had something to do with it," she concluded.

WILBUR J. WILKINSON
One of missing men.

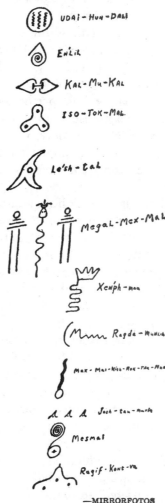

—MIRRORFOTOS

FROM OUTER SPACE?
These weird symbols and words were found on wall of Wilkinson's home. Some have English words penciled lightly beneath. In upper photo, "Lesh-tal," next to last line, is translated "Create Life." Lower, second line, "Xenph-mau" has scribbled under it: "Poseid Returning." Third from bottom, "Josh-tau-marin," is translated: "Births give cataclysms."

23

the activities of the two men, for she had typed up an elaborate report. It introduced a third party, Jerrold Baker, a saucer researcher, who had been personally acquainted with the missing men for many months prior to their disappearance. Manon Darlaine first met Hunrath at George Adamski's house in Palomar Gardens, Calif., in November of 1952. (*The late George Adamski is the author of several books in which he claims to have contacted space people from Venus and other planets. What I hope is a sensible review of Adamski's claims appears later in this book—JWM*).

At that time Baker, Hunrath and a George Williamson were forming the Adamski Foundation, a kind of Grand Authority or clearing house for flying saucer information. Each of these three was to contribute his own special knowledge of UFOs to the Foundation's fund of information. Hunrath qualified, in that he was an electrical engineer; before coming to California he had performed experiments in electromagnetism and had constructed a machine which not only would demonstrate the effects of that phenomena but accomplish remarkably demonstrable results as well.

This machine, contained in a black box, and to which he had given the strange name Bosco was designed in an effort to duplicate the magnetic power by which the saucers were assumed to operate. (One of its more sinister purposes was to create a magnetic fault, which would cause any saucer operation in its proximity to crash in the vicinity of the machine!)

Bosco's contribution to saucer research was soon to run into some snags, however, as The Adamski Foundation became side-tracked into metaphysical rather than mechanical research. And thus began a series of fantastic episodes at Palomar Gardens where Adamski held court and conducted his researches.

Williamson would go into mediumlike trances, and receive space messages, which he would repeat to his listeners in a voice different from his own—as if the space intelligences had taken possession of both his will power *and his vocal chords*. At times he even spoke in unknown languages.

The group would take elaborate notes, make tape recordings of the messages and later try to decipher the information given by Williamson in trance. Later, Williamson would assign pictograph symbols to the languages in the messages, based (he said) on his knowledge of anthropology and ancient symbology.

"Can you give me some details on this?" I asked

Manon Darlain, pointing to her simple note, "Personal falling out."

"I had been sworn to secrecy on this point, and anyhow I don't believe in 'personalities,' but now that Hunrath and Wilkinson have disappeared, maybe I had better clear this up.

"Adamski is peculiar among the crackpots—and I don't mean this in a disparaging way; I'm just using this term as it is used on the West Coast—in that he doesn't go in for any psychic or occult explanations for flying saucers. Although Adamski believes in telepathy, this to him is a purely physical matter, the ability of a superior brain to transmit messages to another brain, electronically. Adamski did not approve of Ric's (Williamson's) trance-mediumship method of obtaining information, and some of the other activities of the threesome, who in my personal opinion, were in part simple freeloaders of Adamski's bed and board, did not meet with his personal approval. The relationships apparently became more strained and the final breakup was precipitated by Hunrath's announcement that he was going to use the Bosco machine to interrupt the magnetic fields of saucers, which appeared regularly over Mt. Palomar, *and bring them down.*

"Adamski, if insincere, would probably not have believed this; instead he became enraged with the idea. He ordered Hunrath to remove the black box from Palomar Gardens—and when the latter refused, an argument ensued and all three guests were ordered to leave the premises." (*Madame Darlain's information once more proves to be valid. A recent book,* Gray Barker's book of Adamski (*Saucerian Books, 1966), presents a lengthy personal letter to the publisher from Adamski in which he elaborates at length on his relationships with Hunrath, the black box, and the argument which ensued—JWM.*

After the schism in The Adamski Foundation, Hunrath, Baker and Williamson went to Los Angeles to seek employment. Since Williamson through his study of anthropology and extensive living among the American Indians, had knowledge of Indian dances, for a while he and Baker considered the idea of performing these dances publicly, with Baker doing the narration. While these two pondered this unique self-imployment, Hunrath with his technical background, obtained a job with an aircraft company. A few months later, Williamson returned to his wife, Betty in Prescott, Arizona.

Baker and Hunrath moved into an apartment in Los Angeles.

The tale hereby began to hang, I gathered from Manon, from the introduction of another character into the bizarre Ufological plot.

"In August, Wilkinson, who had worked with Hunrath in some of his earlier experiments with Bosco, joined him. He had quit a job as foreman at an electrical plant in Racine, Wisconsin, before coming back to L.A. to look up his former buddy.

"Hunrath and Baker introduced the newcomer to Williamson, and Wilkinson also appeared soon to fall under Willianson's spell. The three made several trips to Prescott to confer with Williamson and to listen as he received his mediumistic messages."

I began to suspect that the seed of this weird idea had been planted by Adamski, with his talks of meeting space people. According to Manon, all four of the persons assumed space names: Baker was Markon, Williamson was Mark III, while Hunrath and Wilkinson were content with Firkon and Ramu. The symbols which Williamson had previously begun to assign to his apparent gibberish now started coming to Hunrath and Wilkinson as visions, at any time of the day or night. They began to write down and interpret them.

"At this point Baker's mother became seriously ill," Manon Darlaine continued, emerging from the kitchen with my breakfast. "Baker left the association; and this probably is the reason he is safe today. I learn from my *sources*, however, that he received a letter stating that the writer, which was Wilkinson, had found out definitely when and where a saucer was going to land. The letter asked Baker to hurry back as soon as possible and participate with them in a meeting with the occupants of the craft."

The three were not only invited to meet the saucer occupants, *but to fly away to Mars in the saucer!*

A knock at the door interrupted her remarks. A young man entered and handed her an ink-stained roll of paper. She unrolled a proof of a widely-circulated afternoon newspaper.

KIDNAPED BY SPACE MEN, the headline declared.

Then I realized partly why Manon Darlaine had been free with this somewhat exclusive information: the papers were now on to it and it was *no longer* the hidden property of her Seven Safes.

During my survey of the West Coast Saucer scene I had begun to learn to take no information too seriously, particularly when it involved the so called lunatic fringe. But subsequent investigation has indicated that the Hunrath-Wilkinson disappearance is one of the most puzzling items in that vast lexicon of saucerology—and still remains one of the major unsolved mysteries of the field.

Although many conflicting rumors continue to circulate about the disappearance, there is no definite evidence that Hunrath, Wilkinson, or their plane were ever seen again. One rumor had it that the plane, partly dismantled, was spotted from the air by a search party, but no ground expedition has succeeded in locating it, although a thorough search was made.

Several other facts serve to heighten the baffling mystery. A few weeks after the disappearance, the airport from which Hunrath and Wilkinson rented their plane was destroyed by fire.

The day after the disappearance a peculiar man in a white uniform visited Mrs. Wilkinson and told her that her husband was alive and safe. He gave no details, but did leave his name and address. Baker contacted him, and became convinced that the man did not know anything. Later, other stories circulated, contributing to the idea that the men might still be alive. One such story involved a newspaper ad in the personals column of a Los Angeles newspaper, in which the writer of the ad stated in a cryptic manner that he was interested in saucers and would like to contact like-minded people. Some of the people who had known the missing pair though that Hunrath or Wilkinson had placed the ad in order to contact their friends. Baker also followed up this lead and found the writer to be unconnected with the case. Another story had it that the missing men skipped for Mexico, in an effort to get away from personal problems in California.

Today, looking at the case objectively, the balance of evidence favors the opinion that the men are dead. It is known that Hunrath, who flew the plane, was not an experienced pilot. He had taken a refresher course in flying just the week previous to his disappearance. It is believed that the pair were flying in the direction of Prescott, Arizona, for a saucer rendezvous in that area. This would have taken them over a long stretch of desolate, unexplored country in which there are mountain regions where a plane could crash and not be located for years.

Recently, I came in late to my office and found my secretary, without the usual cheery look on her face. I could sense that she had bad news which she would probably get around to giving me in the afternoon.

Surely enough, in time she handed me a large manila envelope which contained the latest issue of *Saucer News*, my UFO publication. I recognized the envelope as belonging to the usual bundle returned daily by the post office as undeliverable.

Across the face of the envelope was marked the simple word, *Deceased*.

I knew Manon was getting up in years, but I always looked forward to the letter I would always receive commenting on every issue.

No comments, no criticisms, no kudos from this issue. It had been addressed:

Manon Darlaine
P.O. Box 2048-North Wilcox Station
Hollywood 28, Calif.

I knew Pam had not removed this mailing plate from the file, for she had a kind of sixth sense about friends of mine whose mail had become permanently undeliverable.

Two or three days later, late in the evening, I personally would get around to the task.

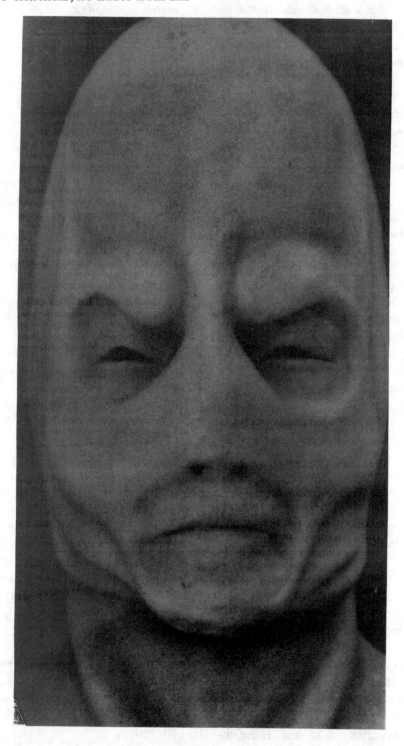

1:45
SCOUT SHIP FROM VENUS

Long John's microphones stand on a long table, above garish, noisy Times Square; yet, high on the 24th floor, with no windows, and sound proofed, the panel member or guest is transported far from the reality of everyday things.

After an hour or so talking on the show you forget you are before microphones. You get the feeling that there is nobody listening and the broadcast becomes almost an unreal thing.

Of course, Long John periodically jokes about his original Society of Eight, the legendary eight listeners who he avers were, at one time the only people tuned in. The truth is that immediately after John went on the air he gathered about a million listeners. In New York, the late movies may drown him out in a few homes, but across the eastern part of the nation truck drivers, travelers and others of a large and avid section of the radio audience regularly lose their sleep listening to Long John's fantastic interviews. It is this wide and enthusiastic audience which gives him his fantastic ratings.

This evening when Yonah opened a large strange book of more than a thousand pages I knew he was ready to make some interesting comments. I leaned over and gleanced at the opened pages of the two-column format with text which read like the Bible.

"This is *Oahspe*, or *New Bible*," Yonah told me off-mike, during a recorded commercial.

I would later know why Gray Barker was obviously trying to avoid the subject of *Oahspe*. As a commercial bookseller, he had offered the book to his customers and sold a number of copies. Although he made a good profit on the high-priced books, the customers; he later told me, often read *Oahspe*, accepted it as the Whole Truth, and would not buy any other books for months—as if they

already had all the answers!

The book, however, as I would learn later, certainly was mysterious enough in its conception and writing, let alone its contents. Its authorship is remarkable in that a human agent transcribed the words, while in trance, at the direction of heavenly beings.

John B. Newbrough was an Ohio boy who came East to enter the dental profession, and soon became one of the leading dentists of New York City.

Newbrough happened one evening to be visiting a circle of friends of social note when the host suggested that one of the guests, who had some fame as a medium, conduct a seance for the group. Newbrough reluctantly assented to join, and then was astounded. Once the seance had begun he found that he could not control his hands, which could not lie on the table without flying into "tantrums", as he put it.

"Often they would write messages, left or right, forward or backward," one of his letters declared.

Newbrough became interested in seances and attended many. He found his strange power growing and his hands continued to move in these tantrums, much to his annoyance at times. When he would control his hands by withdrawing them from the table, the baffling power would attack his tongue, his eyes, or ears, at which times he claimed to hear "differently from my normal state."

Newbrough spent more than twelve years traveling hundreds of miles, investigating various mediums, trying to disprove them. Finally, entirely convinced, he decided he wanted to know more about the spirit world.

The dentist began a series of fasts, frequent bathing, and rising before daybreak for meditation, in an effort to develop his powers.

George Adamski claimed that he met a Venusian space pilot in the desert. He is shown standing beside a painting of the spacemen. The painting was executed by Gay Betts.

According to a letter Newbrough wrote to *The Banner of Light*, Boston, Mass., on Jan. 21, 1883:

"A new condition of control then came upon my hands. Instead of the angels holding my hands as formerly, they held their hands over my head and they were clothed with sufficient materiality for me to see them. And a light fell upon my hands as they lay on the table. In the meantime I was directed to get a typewriter. This I did.

"One morning the light struck both my hands on the back and they went for the typewriter for some fifteen minutes, very vigorously, I was told not to read what was printed, and I had worked myself into such a religious fear of losing this new power that I obeyed reverently. The next morning, also before sunrise, the same power came and wrote again. One morning I accidentally looked out the window and beheld the line of light that rested on my hands extending like a telegraph wire toward the sky. Over my head were three pairs of hands, fully materialized. Behind me stood another angel with her hands on my shoulders. My looking did not disturb the scene.

"For fifty weeks this continued every morning and then it ceased and I was told to read and publish the book *Oahspe*.

Although this was the twentieth century and we were broadcasting from a New York far removed from the days of Newbrough, I remember, as we talked about contactees, thinking that the case of the dentist's visions and contacts were not much different from those of George Adamski, Howard Menger, and the others of the present. Instead of seeing angels, the modern contactees saw spacemen—and *space women*. Maybe it was because of the age involved, a mechanistic one, when man himself was on the threshold of space.

Now it was not so remarkable that Newbrough should see angels, I thought, but that he could come up with such a monumental volume—for sheer size alone! Even though the contents might not be generally accepted, and even though they may have come from his subconscious, as some claimed, his subconscious must have been remarkable.

According to the angels of *Oahspe* (the celestial authors) one of their numbers, Sethantes, was appointed by their government about 79,000 years ago to take charge of the earth and to people it with beings like themselves, capable of immortality. With Sethantes came millions of other space-dwelling entities and they accomplished that mission. They caused a new race of primates to appear here called man—flesh of the earth with an imperishable spirit.

Since that day (all of this still according to *Oahspe* enthusiasts) "the etherean hosts of the Most High," aided by their heirs and successors, have maintained a vigilant jurisdiction over the earth and its inhabitants. Since then, they have never ceased trying to make mankind aware of his dual heritage, trying to make him obedient "to the spirit within" and appreciative of its great possibilities. By phychic means and stratagems they have tried to keep us making progress toward a higher world civilization, and then toward a higher spiritual development.

Flying saucers were not new to the thousands of *Oahspe* students who have studied the book for almost a century. The vehicles that Oahspe ethereans used for travel correspond quite closely with what people are seeing today. Whatever flying saucers are, they certainly are nothing new.

Yonah had brought up the subject of *Oahspe* in order to make a point.

George Hunt Williamson (whom we met in the previous chapter through his associations with Hunrath and Wilkinson) was, according to Yonah, a very serious student of the huge book, and believed practically everything it expounded. Williamson interpreted certain sections as a prophecy for a contact to be made with a spaceman on a certain date—a date which he predicted for George Adamski, who went out onto the desert to help fulfill the prediction.

Yonah held that the entire Adamski affair was a made-up-thing, concocted to make the *Oahspe* prediction come true.

Gray Barker had defended the contactees in some of his publications and books. Yonah's inference was that he also may have had something to do with the Adamski story. This I doubted very much. Probably no reporter or investigator in the field had spent any more effort and time than had I in trying to expose Adamski, the author of three popular books claiming that he had met and talked to men from Venus.

I had been before the Long John microphones on one previous occasion with Adamski, and thoroughly enjoyed interrogating him. In fact I suppose you could say that we had become friends—of sorts—though our beliefs differed.

As I thought of Adamski, I thought of the pleasant evening I had with him back in 1953. I had driven my car up the winding road to the very top of Mt. Palomar in search of him. As I ascended the mountain I mused over the many strange situations I had run into as a result of Manon Darlaine's leads. While I had come to California with the idea of writing an "expose-type" book about the UFO "fringe" crowd, I had run across a lot of exciting material. Maybe it was the heat, maybe it was the emotional climate: but I had to prevent myself from beginning to believe a part of what I'd heard and investigated.

Manon Darlaine had never discussed Adamski at any length. It was not until I was preparing to leave California did I hear the rumor that, if it checked out, could be mighty important—a rumor that there was proof that flying saucers and visiting space people were real!

A Mt. Palomar astronomer, the story went, had come out with a book, published in England, which declared that he had met a Venusian pilot of a saucer on a California desert and talked to the creature with the aid of sign language. The astronomer's name was Professor Adamski.

Not having telephoned ahead, I had some doubts about being able to see the professor, but I had previously found that the best way to see a relatively inaccessible public figure was to show up in his outer office and to talk my way in.

I had met such a figure on my way to California. Stopping off in Independence, Mo., I had been able to walk into former president Harry S. Truman's office and interview him about flying saucers. This interview, however, was less successful than my entrance. In answer to my first question about UFO, Mr. Truman succinctly replied:

"I've never seen a purple cow

.....But I'd rather see than be one."

And with that, my interview came to an end!

Instead of a hard time at the Palomar reception office, I got a horse laugh from a passing staff member when I asked about Professor Adamski.

"The *Professor*," and he emphasized the title in a mocking manner, "lives half way down the mountain. You'll find him running a hot dog stand down there."

The receptionist gave me a more thorough and restrained explanation: No there was no Professor George Adamski at the Observatory: the man I was looking for could be found at Palomar Gardens, a restaurant on the slopes of the mountain which catered to the tourists who came to see the 200-inch telescope at the crest. Yes, Adamski had written a book about flying saucers and had claimed to take photographs of them.

"You'll have to pardon Dr. I'm afraid he can be very blunt at times," she added.

Adamski didn't really own the restaurant, but lived nearby. He spent a great deal of time in the restaurant, however, telling his story to the people who were beginning to flock there to see him. The receptionist herself had stopped by on one occasion, and had found his story most interesting—though she was skeptical about his claims.

I drove back down the mountain to Palomar Gardens and parked in the lot almost filled with cars. Inside I quickly spotted a gray-haired man who appeared to be in his sixties, seated at one of the tables. A crowd of thirty to forty people sat open-mouthed as he related his story.

Adamski did not claim to have any connection with Palomar Observatory. "I am a philosopher, teacher, student, and saucer researcher," he told us. "For several years I have been an amateur astronomer, and have two small telescopes, one of them a 15-inch reflecter, and the other a six-inch refractor."

Long interested in the possibility of life on the other planets, Adamski had written a fictional book wherein interplanetary visitations took place. He had also conducted a school of Tibetan philosophy, known as The Royal Order of Tibet.

His real interest in flying saucers began, Adamski said when two men from the Point Loma Navy Electronics Laboratory, near San Diego, visited him. These men, J.P. Masfield and G.L. Bloom, assured him that the flying saucers were probably interplanetary and that an Earth government was also developing such machines.

The purpose for their visit was to secure his cooperation in photographing the strange craft, on the assumption that his small telescopes could maneuver more easily than the large one at the Observatory. They planned to make a similar request to the Observatory Staff.

Thus, having been asked by the military, as Adamski put it, to cooperate with them, he purchased additional photographic equipment and began to watch the sky for the spacecraft.

"Night after night I stayed outdoors with my telescope aimed, camera attached. Some nights I thought I might freeze because of the cold winds.

"Alice K. Wells, owner of Palomar Gardens, brought hot steaming coffee by the dozens of cups but this was very little comfort. Once I caught an extremely bad cold and was away from my task for weeks while recovering, but still I persisted."

Even though Adamski's liason with the Point Loma technichians soon terminated (for some unexplained reason), he continued his efforts at saucer photography and was rewarded with some sightings and some reasonably good photos—though most of the pictures did not turn out well. Not being a photographer, Adamski had to master the art as he went along. Absolutely convinced of the saucers' reality after the sightings, he began to hope that the time would come when he could make a personal contact with some person from another world. Many times he wandered out onto the desert, feeling he had received telepathic messages from the saucers.

But it was not until November 20, 1952, that Adamski's wish became a reality.

In August, 1952, he had met two Prescott, Arizona, couples, Mr. and Mrs. Bailey, and Dr. and Mrs. George Hunt Williamson. Since the couples were also interested in possible contacts with space people, they asked to be invited to come along the next time he made one of his desert trips. Accordingly, Adamski phoned Williamson on November 18 and arranged to meet the two couples near Desert Center, California, two days later. Adamski's secretary Lucy McGinnis, and Alice K. Wells, were invited to go along.

The seven people met on schedule and proceeded to a point on the highway about eleven miles from Desert Center. The Baileys brought a movie camera, the Williamsons a still camera; Adamski took along his 6-inch telescope, binoculars, and a case containing his still camera and gadgets for attaching it to the telescope. He also had seven cut film holders and an inexpensive camera.

Williamson, who still claimed to be an anthropologist, had even brought along plaster of Paris in case any ground markings needed to be preserved. Thus, the party was quite well prepared in case a meeting with a saucer or a space man should come about.

"The first unusual occurrence," Adamski told us, "was the sighting of a huge mother ship type of saucer, that's the dirigible-looking type, which appeared at a very high altitude and was seen by all our party. We had camped right next to the highway, and I'm sure this mother ship could have been seen by any passing motorist.

"But I had the feeling that this would not be the spot where we might make contact. I had Lucy drive me to a spot a half mile or so from the highway. I then asked her to return and rejoin the others for the period of an hour, after which I would return if nothing had happened. I had a very strong feeling that this would be the day for a contact and that I should be alone."

He set up his telescope and related equipment, and within five minutes was rewarded by the sight of "a small scout ship type of saucer some distance from me. I took seven photos of this ship, though these did not turn out well for some reason.

"Right after this, I saw motion out of the corner of my eye, looked and saw a man approaching me. Although this person looked very much like an ordinary man, he was dressed in a peculiar type of ski suit clothing and had long flowing hair."

To quote from Adamski's book, "The beauty of his form surpassed anything I had ever seen... I felt like a little child in the presence of one with great wisdom and much love, and I became very humble within myself, for from him was radiating a feeling of infinite understanding and kindness, with supreme humility."

Although the story Adamski was telling was fantastic, I was impressed by the many photos, tacked up on the wall, of disc-shaped objects with portholes, dome-type super-structures and spherical landing gear. I also realized almost immediately that I personally liked this man, for he seemed to radiate a humble attitude and good will. Although other members of the restaurant audience became vituperative, including a skeptical heckler who tended to disrupt Adamski's colorful narrative, the "Professor" displayed remarkable patience and interrupted his story to answer his objections and to go into irrelevant details.

Later, when I published many articles critical to Adamski in *Saucer News*, and when I appeared with Long John as a skeptical panelist, Adamski never displayed any personal animosity toward me. Instead he treated me kindly and spoke well of me to others.

Although I have, in later years, become known as one of Adamski's chief critics, I must confess that during this restaurant audience he held me enthralled, as he continued his story:

"The meeting lasted about three quarters of an hour. During this time, by using gestures, I learned that the man was from the planet Venus and that his visit here on Earth was due in part to concern over our use of atomic weapons. To express the idea of atomic explosions, the Visitor said Boom! Boom! Unfortunately, He would not allow me to photograph him. I got the mental impression that perhaps many of these Venusians were already on Earth, mixing with Earth people, and that possibly some distinguishing feature in such a photograph might enable people to identify them more easily."

Toward the end of the interview, the Venusian

made a point of calling Adamski's attention to his footprints in the sand. It developed that the soles of his shoes were inscribed with symbolic markings. After he returned to his scout ship and departed, Adamski rejoined the others and excitedly led them to the scene. Williamson, fully prepared for such an eventuality, made plaster casts of the footprints. Subsequently, many people had tried to interpret the strange symbols impressed by the shoes, but had failed to come up with anything definite.

In the course of his talk with Adamski, the Venusian asked permission to borrow one of Adamski's film packs, with the promise to return it to him shortly. About three weeks later a similar—or the same—scout ship flew over the vicinity of Palomar Gardens, and the pilot dropped the film pack out one of the portholes.

The film, upon development, revealed more strange symbols, similar to those in the footprints. Adamski had a number of language experts at work on the "writing," yet without results—though one of them pointed out that the symbols appeared similar to a language called Urdu, which had been reproduced in a strange book titled *From India to The Planet Mars*, in which a Frenchwoman claimed to have obtained messages from Mars while in trance state.

The next month, December 13, however, Adamski succeeded in getting several good pictures of the scout ships—these were the ones displayed on the wall. Another photo of one of the ships, though blurred, had been made by Jerrold E. Baker, who said he snapped it with a Kodak Brownie camera as the saucer flew away and passed rapidly over the low hill on which he was standing.

Adamski further strengthened his account with a sworn statement made by the witnesses, a photostat of which he took from a brief case and passed around through our group. I copied it after it had finished its full circuit:

I/we the undersigned, do solemnly state that I/we have read the account herein of the personal contact between George Adamski and a man from another world, brought here in his Flying Saucer "Scout Ship," and that I/we was/were a party to and witness to the event as herein recounted.

I was determined to have a private audience with Adamski, so I remained in the restaurant until he had gone through the account at least five times. I must say, however, that this repetition was not particularly boring, for the Professor, though his handling of official Earth Language was unique indeed, delightful—his apparent sincerity and sense of the dramatic made it all worth while.

Each recounting was somewhat different, in that Adamski added details he had not mentioned as the groups who came and went constantly, like the audience at some fantastic grind movie house.

The foregoing is a composite of his various tellings of the story.

When the last of the diehards left the restaurant, including (finally) the lady who imagined that her husband was really a man from outer space and wanted means of positively proving the case. I told Adamski that I was a prospective author of a saucer book. Surprisingly, Adamski took great interest in me and graciously gave all the time I wanted to ask questions. Mostly, however, his end of the conversation was a rehash of what he had already related.

As a very brash, unprofessional and quite naive young man, I'm afraid I asked Adamski:

"Would you tell me honestly, and just between the two of us is all of this the truth—or were you merely writing an exciting book?"

I suppose I wanted him to answer "Yes. It's the truth."

Adamski showed no anger or discomfort at the question. Instead, he put a fatherly arm on my shoulder, led me over to the counter where, finally, after the tedious hours of the lectures, he could relax. He drew a half-filled bottle of vodka from behind the counter, and somebody brought some orange juice. He mixed a screwdriver for both of us, and although I never did like this drink, I enjoyed that one.

Adamski, relaxing still further, departed from the subject of flying saucers altogether, as if, filing away my unanswered question for further reference, he wanted to get away from the general matter. He asked me where I was from, and in a number of other friendly questions, made me feel he was genuinely interested in me.

Warmed by the drink, he raised his eyes to a calendar on the wall, which displayed a well-rounded female, and his eyes twinkled. Then he ripped off a couple of jokes that really shocked me, not because I was unused to such stories or did not thoroughly enjoy them—but because they seemed so much out of context.

"When you are older," he then told me, and a grave look came over his face, "you may learn the truth about the mission of the space brothers. It may be, but I hope that this is not the case, that you will be too old a man, as alas I am, to do much about this.

"What I have told you and the others tonight is absolutely true. But who is it that asked in the poem, 'What is truth?' I don't remember, I am not a literary man. You must not only take my truth, but you must discover the truth for yourself. In that manner, you will truly believe, as I do."

All of this, despite Adamski's charming hospitality, sounded like doubletalk to me; and I have as yet not discovered just what he was getting at—if anything—even though I am much older. And I am still waiting, of course, to see if there was any meaning to a very odd prediction he next made:

"If you don't believe in the space ships," Adamski went on, "and the space brothers, as I don't think you do, young man, wait until 1968 and you will find more understanding—or at the most until 1969."

As I drove down the winding slopes of Mt. Palomar I wondered if he had been predicting something or engaging in occult mumbo jumbo.

The rock 'n roll on the car radio suddenly halted and a voice blurted in, announcing that Soviet scientists had just predicted that artificial satellites would be orbiting the earth by 1957. I laughed. The Soviets were even crazier than anybody I had met on the West Coast.

2:10
THE SAUCER BUG

I had planned to remain in the Los Angeles area for only a week, to gain a general overview of the UFO situation there. Already I had been there fifteen days, yet I decided to check out some of the claims I had heard—particularly those of Adamski, who seemed to be the most important, or at least the most controversial figure I had met.

A good lead might be G.L. Bloom, one of the two men from the Point Loma Navy Electronics Laboratory who, Adamski said, visited him and created his interest in photographing the saucers. In the course of their conversation with him they had also, Adamski alleged, confirmed the landing of a flying saucer in Mexico City.

A telephone call to Bloom brought a very quick denial about part of Adamski's story. He claimed to have no knowledge whatsoever of a Mexico City landing incident. Strangely enough, he would not be specific in confirming or denying that he and the other man had encouraged Adamski. His only positive statement was that "I have been grossly misquoted in *Flying Saucers Have Landed*. Apparently he had seen an advance copy.

Although Bloom's brief testimony certainly did not deny the meeting, the fact that Adamski might embellish the conversation with the Mexico City incident certainly did not put him in favorable light in terms of his total veracity.

I was unable to reach the other man, who Adamski said was J.P. Maxwell.

Another point that troubled my mind was Adamski's remark that if his pictures of saucers were really photos of U.S. secret military aircraft, the Air Force would not have allowed him to distribute them. He said he had sent a complete set to Wright-Patterson Air Force Base, in Dayton, Ohio, scene of the Project Bluebook saucer investigation, and that no interest was taken in

them. Had the photos been genuine space ships, I reflected, surely the Air Force would have been even more interested—and would have requested the negatives for evaluation.

The fact that Adamski had witnesses to his desert contact had been a point which almost clinched my total belief; however this began to slowly fall apart as my visit ran into its third week.

Although at least two of the witnesses were close personal friends and might not be completely impartial (one was the owner of the property where he lived, and the other his secretary); at first glance the other four seemed to be free from prejudices toward spaceship reality.

Dr. George H. Williamson, who had been accompanied by his wife, was impressive—until I remembered that he had been the person involved with Karl Hunrath and had lived at Adamski's place during the incident of the "black box." He had also engaged in telepathic reception of space messages while there, and possibly connected with the Hunrath-Wilkinson disappearance. An anonymous Los Angeles source told me that Dr. Williamson had no doctor's degree; that indeed he had never received a diploma from an undergraduate college, and had in fact been expelled because of poor scholarship. (*This evidence was later formally confirmed in a letter from The University of Arizona, formally signed by a responsible official of the University.*)

A personal visit to Al Bailey, who with Mrs. Bailey, comprised the other two witnesses, convinced me that he had been an ardent believer long before the desert incident. Further, he did *not* see the space man with whom Adamski allegedly talked, nor did he see the scout ship which Adamski said landed. He did, however, see a dirigible-shaped mother ship, and some flashes of light in the direction where Adamski was supposed to be during the contact.

To the best of his knowledge, no one else present saw any more than he did! Furthermore, a drawing, supposedly made by Alice K. Wells while watching Adamski and his visitor through binoculars, could not in his opinion have been made from that distance—about a mile away.

Nevertheless, despite this negative evidence, Bailey *believed* that the contact may actually have taken place, though he personally could not vouch for it.

According to another West Coast informant, it would have been almost impossible for the space man (unless of tremendous weight) to have made such sharp imprints in the sand. There had been no rain for several months and the loose sand would not have received such a definite impression.

I wondered that if the space man were indeed from Venus, how he had been able to defy all scientific evidence by existing so easily and comfortably in Earth's atmosphere, since it is an established fact (confirmed, later, by the Mariner space probes) that the Venusian atmosphere is much different from ours. How, also, did the spaceman defy the laws of probability by looking so much like an Earth man?

Why had no one succeeded in taking any movies or *decent* still pictures of the mother ship seen during the November 20 contact?

Not only did Adamski's story need a great deal of further reappraisal; in fact, almost everything I had seen on the Coast did also.

Probably Gray Barker could fill me in on many of these things, I thought, if I were able to see him on my way back home. Barker had put me off when I had called him earlier, with the excuse that he was departing on a three-week trip to the southern part of West Virginia to act as a consultant for a school system which was making a film. I suspected that he simply did not want to see me. On the phone he seemed somewhat nervous speaking to me.

I remembered, however, that Dominick Lucchesi and August C. Roberts had been suspicious of me when I visited them, until they talked with me for a while and became convinced I was not one of the Three Men in Black!

By now, or more likely five minutes after my visit to Augie and Dom had ended, they had probably been on the phone to Barker giving him a report on me. Since there must have been some contact since then, Barker probably now knew that

I was not somebody coming to shush him up, seize his files, or do any of the other half-feared, half-hoped-for misfortunes which I found so many saucer enthusiasts expected would soon happen to them.

This time, my phone call to Barker drew a much more favorable response. He invited me to stop at his apartment and invited me to stay overnight. I declined, but made an appointment to see him for an hour or so.

I was reminded of the story of the missing film when I saw how the drive-in theatre industry had apparently made Barker most affluent.

In his letters he had just moved from a rooming house to a beautiful apartment which he had just furnished, and now had his own private office.

At his apartment Barker spent an hour subjecting me to demonstrations of his high-fidelity record player and color television sets, two items which, at that date, were quite novel.

Whenever our talk finally settled down to UFOs Barker became noticeably nervous and fidgety. He pulled out a large file of letters, reports and correspondence—from and regarding the International Flying Saucer Bureau—most of which were letters to and from the director, Albert K. Bender.

I'm trying to put all this together, but somehow it just doesn't make sense," he stated.

Barker finally revealed that he had been visited by the FBI before Bender's hush-up, and he believed that the visit had something to do with the Bender mystery.

A man from out of town, being treated in a local hospital, had in his possession a business card issued by the IFSB, and having heard of Barker's interest in saucers had come to get information from him.

Barker did not know how the man could have got hold of the card, since he had just received his package of cards a few days before. "Did the FBI investigators discourage your investigation?" I asked.

"No, and that's peculiar, if it has anything to do with Bender. They just asked a few questions about the organization, and if I knew this chap, and that's all. I guess I must have got overly frightened for I should have asked *them* some questions. But I had never before been visited by the FBI and was very nervous."

Barker had pulled out all of his files on the IFSB and was trying to search out the possible "answer" that Bender had come up with before being visited by the men who had confirmed the information

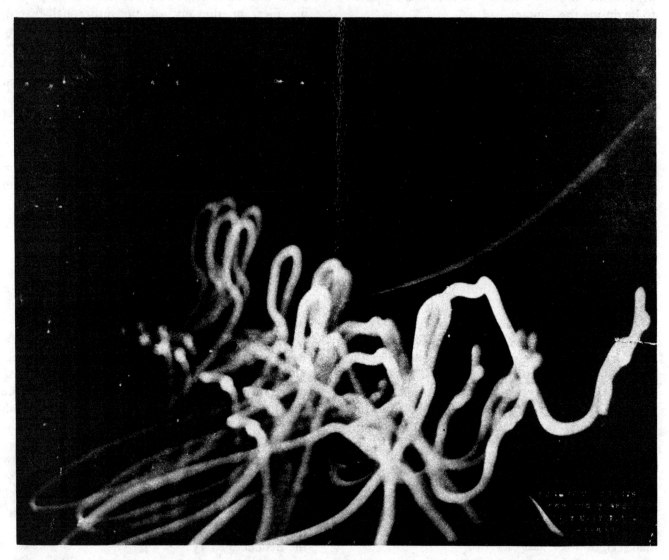

One of the classic UFO photos of all time was this one taken by August C. Roberts, from a Ground Observer's platform in New Jersey during 1952. Roberts opened the shutter to reproduce the movements of the strange object. The object was witnessed by hundreds of people in the area. (Photo courtesy August C. Roberts)

and offered even more. Also he was beset with some devils of doubt, and was wondering whether or not Bender was telling the truth.

Worst of all, Barker feared he would be interfered with in some way and wondered if he should stop his investigations and the publication of a small magazine, *The Saucerian* which he had just begun.

"I'm truly fascinated by the study of UFOs and I don't want to stop. Yet if it's something the government doesn't want me to do, as a loyal citizen I would give it up."

Barker had just received a review copy of Adamski's *Flying Saucers Have Landed*. A skim reading disclosed that it followed essentially the same story I had heard from the author. Most of the pictures I had already seen at Palomar Gardens.

"I don't know quite what to think of Adamski's

part of the book," Barker told me, "but Desmond Leslie's part is tremendous."

He was referring to the fact that the book was really written by two different authors, the part by Adamski comprising approximately half the volume, after a long introduction by Desmond Leslie.

Leslie's contribution consisted mainly of a history of flying saucers, from which he drew largely on the works of Charles Fort, the books Dom and Augie had acquainted me with. Going into old manuscripts, however, Leslie came up with what seemed to me very wild interpretations of some of the ancient Indian poetry, which, according to Leslie, was filled with flying saucers, the "magic carpets" of those ancient days.

"I think that the subject of flying saucers has great occult significance," Barker interjected during my comments on the book. "From my contacts in the field it seems that people who are interested in occult matters such as Yoga, ESP, ceremonial magic and the like are also tremendously interested in UFOs. With me, it's the other way around. I'm now trying to find out all I can about the occult."

Although Barker had been very helpful, had given me much material, and cleared up some of my questions about the field, I remember that I could not help being disappointed by his preoccupation with the Three Men In Black story, and by his interest in occult subjects which I felt had no part in an objective investigation.

This was my last stop driving back to New York, so as I maneuvered my Ford around the twisting West Virginia roads, I began to think back and review my trip.

Barker's account of the closing of the saucer organization and Bender's strange visitors in black, (the same story told by Dom and Augie) was most dramatic, and even entertaining. And Barker's sincerity was, like Adamski's, convincing.

But what facts had I really learned about the case? The information was mainly second hand, *and Bender had not disclosed the identity of the men who discouraged him.*

What facts had I really obtained in any of my investigations?

The story that Mortimer Bane had told me included, as proof, a piece of engraver's metal with deep scratches on it. True, the lab report looked authentic, but the mark need not have been made by a Venusian's fingernail, but by a hoaxer's machine tool.

Since the film which the air force had allegedly confiscated was still confiscated it could not be proven that the movie had ever been taken at all. I had only the producer's word for it.

The only proof existing in the strange Hunrath-Wilkinson case was the fact that they were still missing. They could have been whisked away to Mars, could have crashed in the mountains—or maybe they took a powder to Mexico.

My strange interview with Dom and Augie, prior to my West Coast trip, had contained little more than wild claims about a possible earth tilt, saucers coming from inside the earth, and other assorted information of similar value.

The writing of a book, such as Krippene had suggested, however, which made fun of the crackpots of California, was repugnant to me. Whether they were crackpots, seers, or frauds, I found that I had liked most of these people I had interviewed and investigated.

Most of them, especially Adamski, expressed philosophies of peace and the brotherhood of man, ideals of some value, even if they had been received from space people from the mouth of the Big Dipper itself. The majority of the "contactees" were kind, friendly people.

The "saucer bug" had bitten me. Although my California visit had left me skeptical and disillusioned, I was slowly reaching the conclusion that there must indeed be something behind all of the reports, particularly some claims by airline pilots which Barker had shown me. If, out of a thousand crackpots, only one of them had actually seen a machine from outer space, here was a man who should be heard. In any case, my research had led me into many interesting situations and created dozens of valuable friendships.

I had just read a book by Major Donald E. Keyhoe who claimed that the United States Air Force knew what the flying saucers really were, but had classified the information and was withholding it from the American public. Was Keyhoe the true prophet of the space age, as many believed? Or was he, like the others, a prophet without substance? Though I frankly expected to learn nothing, I decided to take a short cut and seek my information direct from the horse's mouth—a winged horse, the USAF itself!

The Air Force would open its files to me, then snap them shut, right on my figurative fingers! I would run into more mysterious people with even more mysterious ploys.

Most everybody engaged in civilian saucer research would think that I was secretly on the payroll of the Air Force. This rumor has persisted so widely that at times I have been half-ready to believe it myself—but I'm still waiting for my first check!

2:35
THE AIR FORCE FILES

'Jim, I'd like to ask *you* a question. This has been on my mind for some time because this had been kicked around and kicked around. We've heard so many rumors about James Moseley.

"Is there *any truth* to the story that you are employed by the United States Government; that you are a member of the Air Force, or that you *have* been a member of the Air Force, and that it has been your job to kill the contactee stories in any way that you can, by appearing on radio programs, television programs, and printing brochures?"

Long John Nebel had suddenly turned the interrogation from Gray Barker to me. I was surprised at this. In the past John had helped me field such questions. I had assumed he thought I just might be a secret Air Force representative and was giving me a chance to cover it up.

I knew what Barker was ready to bring up at the drop of a hat from the Three Men In Black incident. While he didn't believe that I was employed by the government to kill the saucer mystery, he wasn't quite sure whether or not I had ever been in the Air Force. One of his investigators had written the AF and received a very confusing letter about a James Mosley (the name spelled slightly differently) who had indeed once served with that branch.

John might be serious in his questioning—or he might be giving me a chance to throw in a note of mystery. Anyhow I decided to play it safe and field the question by saying it wasn't relevant to the evening's discussion whether or not I had ever served in the Air Force. (By avoiding the question about employment by the government, I left this open to even more doubt. I was beginning to enjoy the many rumors going around.)

Gordon H. Evans, a New York executive and expert on far eastern politics, had, on more than one occasion, insisted to my face that I was employed by the CIA—and I couldn't convince him otherwise! This is understandable—I have come to believe that Evans, himself, is a CIA member—and so the suspicions run in the flying saucer field.

But then there are the strange *little* things, like the letter Barker had just published, at the time of this broadcast. It was on official stationery and no doubt authentic.

Now, though I may never be able to convince some of my readers that I have never served in the Air Force, I, myself, know that I haven't.

Several months before the broadcast an anonymous correspondent had written Roger Pierce and Howard Neuberger, editors of the UFO magazine *Cosmic News*, including a strange and ridiculous detail about my hiding behind a counter in a department store! It also claimed that I had been in the Air Force.

I could detect that Barker, not too serious at the moment, was getting a kick out of belaboring the Air Force rumor, and that he was going to ask permission to read the latest letter. John assented and Barker read it.

DEPARTMENT OF THE AIR FORCE
WASHINGTON

OFFICE OF THE SECRETARY   6 July 1959

Dear Mr. Ogden:

Reference a letter from this office to you dated 23 June 1959.

We have obtained more information concerning a James W. Moseley from the Air Reserve Records

Center which follows:

The Air Reserve Records Center does not have a record of 1st Lt James W. Moseley, New Jersey, but a check shows Captain James W. Moseley's name changed to Captain James W. Mosley, A0-2089932, last address Florida. Officer discharged effective 18 December 1957, per Reserve Order 173, dated 1 December 1957.

We do not know if this is the same person you were inquiring about. •

If we can be of assistance, please let us know.

Sincerely,
(Signed) James M. Dyer
Lt. Colonel, USAF
Chief, Reserve Forces Liaison
Office of Information Services

As Barker read the letter I thought about the average person's reaction to it. The coincidence was too great! And there was the business about the spelling of my last name, always a sensitive point to anyone whose name is constantly misspelled.

Was *somebody* consciously and deliberately trying to perpetuate this rumor? If so, the Air Force would have to be in on it. I would think of this again when, in 1959, the infamous Straith Letter to George Adamski, allegedly written on official U.S. State Department stationery—but obviously spurious—was the main subject for discussion in UFO circles. Both Barker and myself were accused of having been behind the letter, much to our discomfort and embarrassment. (*For a complete report on this and other letters which were apparent hoaxes, but as yet unexplained, see* The Book of George Adamski, *Saucerian Books, 1966.*)

Although I have subsequently visited the Air Force Information Desk at the Pentagon a number of times, and have even, later, visited the sacrosanct confines of Project Bluebook at Wright Patterson Air Force Base, my first contact with the AF proved to be the most fruitful, so far as saucer data was concerned.

I often suspect that the chief gripe of spies, when they get together to talk shop, is not the quality of U.S. Government security in Washington. Their beef probably is that simply *finding* the locations of the departments or offices in the Pentagon is more difficult than the actual heisting or microfilming of military secrets!

In my own experience, obtaining secret saucer information from the Air Force was much, much easier than simply finding the Public Information Office. Maybe *that* is why the Public is not informed about the reality of flying saucers!

I had gone to the Pentagon in the late fall of 1953 expecting to be rebuffed, for Major Donald E. Keyhoe (U.S.M.C. Ret.), in his book, *Flying Saucers From Outer Space*, had told how, in the beginning of his research, the AF had given him data on reported sightings but had later clammed up and classified all of the UFO information.

In fact, when I was admitted to the office of Lieutenant (later Major) R.C. White, the information officer at that time, I was surprised to receive a very friendly reception.

"I'm writing a book about flying saucers," I explained (although I had given up on the book, I still found this excuse a wonderful door opener). I know your files are secret, but. . ."

"Now who told you that, old buddy?" the lieutenant interrupted with a big smile, rising and walking to some filing cases. He pulled out several bulging file folders and bound material and handed it over.

"How's this for a starter?" and he gave me a slap on the shoulder. As I slowly opened the folder and peered inside, out of the corner of my eye I could see him pause to light his pipe while he observed my reaction with a quizzical look on his face.

I was so nonplussed that my grip on the bulky folder slipped, and its contents spilled, with a dozen or so Air Force flying saucer sightings falling all over my lap and onto the floor.

"Aren't these classified?" I blurted.

"I was sort of pulling your leg. I'll explain the situation," White replied. "You came in at the right time. You're in for a bit of luck. We've decided to make all of these Status Reports available to interested members of the press and public. In fact it was just last week that this policy was decided upon. We didn't make any federal case out of it with the press, so few people know about it. In fact you're the first person from the saucer press to drop in since this policy went into effect."

I asked him about Major Keyhoe's assertion that the files had earlier been open to him. White explained that although the major had access to most of the information, he had never seen the actual files, the reports either having been transcribed for him, or read to him orally.

"Some people make too big a thing out of their claims about Air Force secrecy. True, these reports haven't been available in the past. Frankly this saved us a lot of trouble with kids and crackpots running in here asking us to see little green men they said we had captured."

Both of us had a laugh.

"Can I—*use* this information?" I asked, still incredulous.

"If you wish you can borrow one of these broken down G.I. typewriters and copy anything you please. Spend as much time as you want. We can't let the reports leave the Pentagon, but they're public information now and you're welcome to copy and use as much as you want."

There was but one restriction:

"I must ask you that in the interest of privacy of witnesses involved that you not use their names, unless, of course, the case and the names are previously known to you. You'll be sort of on your honor there, I suppose."

To have copied everything made available to me would have taken several days. I settled for transcribing only the most dramatic material, and this now occupies more than twenty single-spaced typewritten pages in a private notebook of mine. This is a story I have never revealed during more than ten years of saucer research.

As I copied the reports on the old Underwood, I thought how different they were from the wild stories, supported mainly by rumor, which I had collected in California. In fact a quick look at these Air Force files began to revive my respect for the possible reality of the UFOs.

Here, for example, was a report of a saucer which left contrails! It was observed by military pilots. This and the other reports presented here are printed, with a few minor deletions as we will explain later, exactly as given me by Lieutenant White:

Luke AFB, Arizona—March 3, 1953. In this instance, the object was never observed, but a high altitude condensation pattern was observed. When first sighted, the contrail was approximately 300 to 500 feet in diameter. The pattern began with a smooth knife-like leading edge, very thin in depth and with an irregular trailing edge. As the source gave chase, the contrail made a slight dip to the NW and began climbing at 20 degrees. During this maneuver, source and object were at right angles, and he observed the pattern to appear as a sharp-nosed, very thin object about 300 to 500 feet long with an irregular, wispy trailing edge. Immediately, a heavy condensation trail began to form and extended for approximately 1000 feet back, at which point it separated into a double trail which again was approximately 1000 feet long, ending abruptly. At this time, the object was traveling at an estimated 400 mph true air speed. The most unusual feature was that the contrail stayed with the unsighted object, and did not extend across the sky as in the case of conventional aircraft contrails. . .The contrail was observed by the pilots of three F-84 aircraft, with only one giving chase. This pilot chased the contrail for fifty to sixty miles before breaking off. . .During the chase, this pilot took approximately thirty feet of gun-camera film. This film was received in very good condition, and had been analyzed by the photographic laboratory at Wright Patterson Air Force Base. Their conclusions are:

(a) The white streak photographed is probably a vapor trail from a rapidly moving object of unknown velocity. The object itself is invisible in the photographs. (b) The exhaust vapor trail, apparently from a twin propulsion unit, is more pronounced at the end of the film. The configurations in the trail appear to be due to maneuvers performed by the object. (c) An additional vapor trail, thought to be due to lifting surfaces, is also in evidence, but it dissipates rapidly. This additional vapor trail appears to be centered about the exhaust trail. (d) Within the period of the time represented by the film, the photographic plane may have reduced the distance between the object and itself. However, the flight paths are not parallel by a considerable angle, so that the object's distance and velocity with respect to the plane cannot be determined with useful precision.

Since there was nothing gained by the photo-analysis, that would actually aid in identifying the object involved, this report is being sent to the Aircraft Laboratory of WADC for further analysis. Until the report is returned from WADC, this incident will be carried by Project Blue Book as unknown.

Conclusion: Unknown

Another report which deeply impressed me involved sightings by visual and radar means:

Continental Divide, New Mexico—January 26, 1953. On January 26, 1953 at 2115 MST Air Force personnel stationed at an AC&W station in this area observed an aerial phenomenon simultaneously by electronic and visual means. To the naked eye the object appeared to be a very bright reddish-white object estimated to be ten miles west of the radar site. The object passed behind a hill and then reappeared apparently heading in a northerly direction at a slow speed. The airmen making this visual observation reported it to personnel manning the radar equipment. They stated that they had an unidentified blip on the radar scope, appearing west of the station approximately nine miles away. The scope showed the object to be on a 270 degree azimuth at an altitude of 10,000 to 15,000 feet, moving away from the site at 12 to 15 mph. It was eventually lost on radar at the eighteen-mile range. The object was under visual and radar observation intermittently for forty-five minutes. The elevation of the station is 7,500 feet above sea level. Weather at the time was characterized by a high thin overcast and low scattered clouds. Winds aloft were from 270 degrees at 30 knots at 10,000 to 30,000 feet. An atmospheric inversion layer existed at 18,000 feet with the top at 21,000 feet.

[This is the most complete report ever received by ATIC (Air Technical Intelligence Command) on the sighting of an unidentified object. . . . . . The combination visual-electronic sighting is the best type to work with because it affords the most information.]

Conclusion: Unknown

Or consider this dramatic close-up sighting, reported by civilians:

Craig, Montana—at 4 A.M., January 3, 1953. Three sources observed an aerial object 25 to 40 feet long and 18 to 25 feet thick with the appearance of two soup bowls put together. There were several lighted windows with what appeared to be a porthole on the side. The object moved slowly at first, then began to climb rapidly. The manner of disappearance was unspecified. The object first appeared at 200 to 300 yards from the observers at an altitude of 10 to 15 feet. An investigation of the sources revealed that they are mature, reliable, and in at least one case, a relatively experienced person.

Conclusions: Unknown

Sightings by Airline Pilots came in for many good reports, as the following:

Minneapolis, Minnesota—The only information available on this incident is this letter. "Time: 6:30 A.M., October 11, 1951. Dick and I were flying at 10,000 feet when I saw a brightly glowing object to the southeast of the University of Minnesota Airport. At that time we were a few miles north of Minneapolis and heading east. I pointed it out to Dick, and we both made the following observations. The object was moving from east to west at a high rate of speed and a very high

altitude. We tried keeping our ship on a constant course and using the reinforcing member of the windshield as a point. The object moved past this member at about 50 degrees per second. This object was peculiar in that it had what can be described as a halo around it with a dark undersurface. It crossed rapidly and then slowed down and started to climb slowly in lazy circles. The pattern it made was like a falling oak leaf, inverted. It went through these gyrations for a couple of minutes and then with a very rapid acceleration disappeared in the east. Dick and I watched this object for approximately five minutes. I can't describe its size. Shortly after this we saw another one, but this one didn't hang around. It approached from the west and disappeared to the east. Neither object left any trace of vapor trail."

Status of Investigation: Observers were positive of the following facts: (A) The object, though vaguely defined and blurred, retained a definite shape. (B) No vapor trails, exhaust flashes, or jet propulsion were observed. (C) The object definitely seemed to be controlled. The sources are experienced engineers with General Mills balloon projects and have been observing all types of balloons for several years.

Conclusions: No conclusions can be made. It is significant, however that the sources can be graded as very reliable and that they observed an object with which they were entirely unfamiliar.

Another combination visual-radar sighting, involved an aircraft scramble to intercept a saucer, was typical of the many similar exciting accounts:

Heneda Air Force Base, Japan. The object was first noticed by two airmen walking across the ramp at Heneda on the night of August 5, 1952 at 11:01 local time. The airmen were on their way to the tower to relieve the operators. On reporting to the tower, the object was called to the attention of the tower operators who were going off duty.

The four operators agreed that the object, which they observed from 50 minutes to an hour through 7 x 50 binoculars, was circular in shape with a distinct brilliance. The light appeared to be a portion of a large, round dark shape which was about four times the diameter of the light. When the object was close enough for details to be seen, a smaller, less brilliant light could be seen along the lower edge of the dark shape. The object faded to the east twice but reappeared; it could have faded or actually gone away and come back. The size of the light, when closest to the tower, was approximately the same as the ceiling balloons that are released near the tower. A comparison was made of these 24 foot diameter balloons at 2000 feet. This would make the object fifty feet in diameter at 10 miles. During the observation, a lighted balloon was released but this light was extremely dim and yellow compared to the object. An airborne C54 was requested to check the object, which the pilot did, but he reported seeing only a star. The AC&W unit was notified soon after the original visual sighting and shortly after 11:51 picked up an unidentified return (on radar). The object was tracked at varying speeds from hovering to 300 knots. At 1:12 A.M. the return *"broke into three pieces"* and they maintained intervals of 1/4 mile. No visual observation was made from the AC&W unit although it was attempted and, at one time, the object was within 10 miles of the station. The radar was directed onto the target by visual observations from the tower, so it can safely be assumed that both visual and radar contacts involved the same object. At three minutes after midnight a fighter was airborne on a scramble and was requested to search the area northeast of Haneda Air Force Base. They could make no visual observations, but could see the north star and Venus. The fighter was vectored to the object by GCI (both the fighter and the object were in the scope), and held for 90 seconds. Shortly after this, both the object and the fighter disappeared into the ground clutter on the radar scope. At no time did the fighter make visual contact. Soon after the loss of the radar contact, the object was lost visually.

Conclusion: Unknown

That the Air Force is without a sense of humor is disproved by the following, which I toss in as an example of an AF conclusion that few can disagree with:

Friona, Texas-November, 1952. Source supposedly picked up pieces of an exploded "flying saucer" and sold half the pieces to the Soviet Embassy. He had previously notified the Pentagon, but hadn't heard from the Pentagon so he sold out to the Soviets.

Discussion of Incident: It is believed that this is a "crackpot" report. The original report was made to the F.B.I. and forwarded to the Air Technical Intelligence Command.

Conclusion: Hoax

The previous cases were taken from a file known as *Project Blue Book Status Report No. 7.* The information on the cover of *Report No. 9,* which I also saw, and which contained similar cases, read: *Confidential Security Information. Status Report. Project Blue Book—Report No. 9—Air Technical Intelligence Center, Wright-Patterson Air Force Base, Ohio—Confidential.*

Most people who are seriously interested in the UFO phenomena have actually read only one of these reports, known as *Project Blue Book Report No. 14.* This was made available to the public, and through the efforts of a private individual, an offset reprint, with some additional notes by the publisher, was produced and sold. *Report No. 14* contains the famous "Twelve Best Sightings," or, in other words, twelve saucer reports which were the most real, factual, and the most puzzling to the Air Force. (*The Twelve Best Sightings Appear in a succeeding chapter.*)

But the liberality with information did not last long at the Pentagon, mainly because of in-fighting by one of the best known saucer researchers in the nation.

After copying what I considered the most convincing sightings, I started going over my material and in the course of my research reread sections of Adamski's *Flying Saucers Have Landed.* Noting that the author had claimed to have had certain conversations with Al Chop, a former civilian member of the Air Force Press Desk at the Pentagon, then residing in Los Angeles, I decided to call him up and check Adamski's claims.

Since he had written a controversial letter to Major Keyhoe which he allowed him to use on the jacket of *Flying Saucers From Outer Space,* I also wanted to tell him the good news about the declassification of the Air Force reports.

As to Adamski, Chop claimed to have been grossly misquoted in the book. When I told him about seeing the Status Reports, however, I heard a little gasp, and for a few seconds there was complete silence at the other end.

"You mean they let you *copy* these? he asked, somewhat incredulously; then he questioned me at length. Somehow he didn't seem too happy about the entire affair.

"You should be informed that you have seen classified information, and I would caution you not to use it," he told me.

Later, I learned, he wrote to the Air Force Press Desk and also to Major Keyhoe. I don't know what he told them, but Keyhoe immediately phoned the Pentagon, complaining that I had been allowed to see information which had been withheld from him.

On December 28, 1953, I received the following letter which is still in my files. The letterhead is the Department of Defense, Office of Public Information, Washington, 25, D.C.:

Dear Mr. Mosely:

We are in receipt of information indicating that you are in possession of classified information concerning radar sites and operating capabilities, and that you are citing this office as your source.

As we pointed out to you, while information concerning actual sightings is not classified, information concerning radar, electronics equipment, and aircraft operating capabilities is classified.

If any of this type of information has been available to you inadvertently or otherwise through this office, I respectfully request that you get in touch with me at the earliest possible moment so that we can determine if any security is involved.

Sincerely,
MONCEL A. MONTS
Lt. Col. USAF
Chief, Air Force Press Desk

At the end of the Christmas and New Year holidays, I drove to Washington to find out what the letter was all about.

Lieutenant White, obviously embarrassed, but without any good reasons to give me as to why, informed me that the Status Reports had been "temporarily removed," supposedly just to have the SECRET and CONFIDENTIAL labels crossed off—since he still insisted that the sighting reports

NEWSFLASH!

A retired professor from the University of South Florida, Professor Robert Carr, claims the United States Air Force secretly recovered the bodies of 12 crew members aboard a UFO that crashed in 1948. Professor Carr says the UFO crashed at an undisclosed location in the United States. He claims that UFO crew members apparently died during a decompression accident. Carr says that autopsies were performed on the human-like beings. He says they were three to four feet high…had yellow to whitish short hair…whitish tan in color with blue eyes. The autopsies reportedly showed an advanced number of convolutions in the brains of the UFO crew members. Convolutions are usually associated with age or advanced intelligence. Professor Carr claims the U.S. Air Force has two spaceships under maximum security. The one that carried the UFO crew members undamaged except a broken window which caused the decompression deaths…and a second UFO which was heavily damaged. But Carr claims that's only a fragment of the story. Professor Carr says because of Watergate, the Nixon administration would do nothing about the UFO issue. But Carr says with a new president in power, a new era of openness in government, the full story should be told to the American people.

Carr claims editors all over the country have told him there will be a change in the government position towards UFOs announced in December. And Carr says the NBC television network has scheduled a documentary on UFOs for Sunday, December 15th.

Professor Carr says an organization he belongs to, known as Science Conferences, will meet November first through the third in Tampa, Florida, urging the administration to tell the people the truth. Carr says Americans are already aware that the U.S. is engaged in a two billion dollar project seeking life on other planets, most notably Mars. He also says Americans are aware of the existence of giant radio telescopes scanning space for life signals. Carr also claims the existence of 12 UFO crew members killed in 1948 is openly discussed in the academic world.

Carr says he himself worked as a member of the National Investigating Committee on Aerial Phenomenon, which is a private civilian group. Carr disputed claims that the committee is a CIA front organization. Carr was asked about identifying the sources of his information regarding the UFO that crashed four years ago. He said that those who have given him the information are either military personnel or civilian scientists sworn to secrecy under the official secrets act. Carr claims the government can no longer sustain an awkward, costly cover-up about the UFO sightings because too many people have seen the UFOs.

Again, Carr claims the government will make a major announcement about UFOs and the United States policy towards them in December.

themselves were not classified.

I felt sorry for White, who had been so kind and cooperative. I felt that he might have inadvertently goofed in giving me the files to copy, so at his suggestion I wrote the following letter, dated January 22, 1954, which was filed at the AIR Force Public Information Office:

TO WHOM IT MAY CONCERN:

There has apparently been some speculation as to the nature of certain material I received from the Air Force Press Desk in November 1953, concerning "flying saucers." The Status Reports made available to me had previously been shown to other interested persons—such as newsmen, etc. These Reports were at that time available to *anyone* sufficiently interested in "saucers," and they definitely were not classified. The only information I received from these Reports that could possibly be construed as classified was as follows: In a few cases the type of radar set was named, and in one or two cases the operating capabilities of radar was referred to. The value of these cases to my forthcoming book is in no way diminished by the omission of this radar information, and I will voluntarily withhold this information when I write up the cases for my book.

I have been very pleased with the help and co-operation given me by the Air Force Press Desk throughout my enquiry into the "flying saucer" phenomenon. However, I want to emphasize again that to the best of my knowledge I have not been granted any special favors, and specifically, I have been shown no documents not available to anyone ambitious enough to walk into the Public Information Office and ask for them.

James W. Moseley

Since the book I referred to was never written in its original form, that was one reason these files have not been printed until this time. As for Lieutenant White, many ardent anti-Air Force saucer fans might criticize me for going to such lengths to get him off the hook. All I can say is that I did not want to see a man penalized for having cooperated with me, and in the back of my mine was the thought that Major Keyhoe was a much more powerful man than I had realized and that he may have been responsible for the clamp-down on public information from the Air Force.

In fact, this incident marked the beginning of the less-than-friendly nature of the relations between myself and Keyhoe, and later between myself and his organization, NICAP. (*The National Investigations Committee on Aerial Phenomena, Washington, D.C.*)

As for the classified information, it is now more than ten years old, and after elimination of information regarding capability of radar and speeds of aircraft, could be of no value to an enemy. I therefore have published these accounts without fear that I have violated security in any way.

THE PUZZLED PROFESSORS

I had made one exception to keeping the information from the Air Force files under wraps. In the November, 1954, issue of Saucer News, I would carry the brief announcement that I was unable to publish the "irrefutable documented evidence" I had promised in a previous issue.

That, of course, is another story, which I will attend to in a succeeding chapter.

As I was editing the issue in which I made the Announcement, I decided I should at least give my readers something which had been in my possession for some time, but never released: the official ATIC Project Bluebook Status Report on the Lubbock lights.

This report, along with the others reproduced in the preceding chapter, had been given to me to copy at the Pentagon.

Of the many cases I had in the Status Reports, this was among those which had impressed me the most. It concerned one of the best publicized sightings in the history of flying saucers. The story and associated photographs had appeared in *Life* Magazine, the best-selling Adamski book, *Flying Saucers Have Landed*, and many other media.

Here, with only minor editing for the sake of clarity, is the text of the Air Force report:

Lubbock, Texas, August 30, 1951: The first of a series of sightings related to this incident occurred on the evening of August 25, 1951, at approximately 9:10 P.M., Central Standard Time. Four Texas Technical College professors were sitting in the back yard of one of the professor's homes, observing meteors in conjunction with a study of micrometeorites being carried out by the college.

At 9:20 P.M. they observed a group of lights pass directly overhead from north to south. The lights had about the same intensity as high cirus clouds on a moonlight night. The altitude of the lights was not determined, but they traveled at a high rate of speed. The pattern of the lights was almost a perfect semi-circle containing from 20 to 30 individual lights. Later in the evening a similar incident was observed, and during a period of about three weeks a total of approximately 12 such flights were observed by these men.

The observers included: Professor W.L. Ducker, PhD, Head of the Petroleum Engineering Department; Dr. W.I. Robinson, PhD, Professor of Geology: and Dr. A.G. Oberg, PhD, a Professor of Chemical Engineering. An unnamed Professor of Mathematics and a graduate student of Texas College were among the other witnesses on the campus, and in addition, over one hundred residents of the town observed the lights at one time or another.

These professors took a personal interest in the phenomena and undertook a study of the object. Attempts were made to obtain an altitude measurement by laying out a measured base line perpendicular to the usual flight path of the object, and placing angle measuring devices at the end of the base line. All these attempts failed because the lights did not appear on the nights the professors were waiting for them with this equipment.

However, from the series of visual observations, they obtained the following facts: (a) The angular velocity of the object was very nearly *30 degrees of arc per second* (italics mine), i.e., from horizon to horizon in about six seconds. (b) The flight path of the object was from north to south in the majority of flights although some were from northeast to southwest. (c) There was no sound that could be attributed to the object. (d) The color of the lights was blue-green. (f) There were 15 to 30 separate lights in each formation. (g) The first two flights observed were a semi-circle of lights but in subsequent flights there was no orderly arrangement. (h) The object always appeared at an angle of about 45 degrees from the horizon in the north, and disappeared at about 45 degrees in the south, i.e., the object did not come gradually into view as would an aircraft approaching from a distance, nor did it disappear gradually. (i) There was no apparent change of size as the object passed overhead.

Attempts were made by the professors to obtain the relative height of the object in respect to the clouds, but were unsuccessful because the object passed between widely scattered clouds. Attempts were made to determine whether or not there was any form between the lights by trying to see stars between the lights. These attempts were also unsuccessful due to the short time the object was in view.

(*Note: A clue to the solid nature of this phenomenon may have been revealed by the Air Force chronicler's unconscious use of the word "object" rather than "objects" in describing this series of lights. Also, this same Status Report describes a sighting which occurred a few miles from Lubbock, on August 25, 1951, in which a low-flying unidentified flying wing type aircraft was sighted in daylight by two people. The shape and lighting of this flying wing was sufficiently similar to the Lubbock affair to cause the Air Force writer to state that a tie-in between the two incidents is considered likely.—JWM*)

On the evening of August 31, 1951, at about 11:30 Central Standard Time, a Texas College freshman named Carl Hart Jr. observed a flight of the unidentified objects fly over his home in Lubbock. The flight was observed through an open window. Upon observing the first flight of these lights, Hart obtained his camera and went into the back yard of his home in an attempt to get photographs of additional flights. Two more flights allegedly did occur and were photographed by him; two photos of one flight and three of another were obtained. The Air Technical Intelligence Center has four of the negatives but the other one was lost or misplaced by the photographer. (*Note: Since this report was written, the Air Force has returned the negatives to Hart*). The photographs show a V-shaped formation of lights. In one photo a single V of lights appear, while on three other photos there is a double-V. The separate lights, which

appear to be pinpoint light sources, vary in intensity.

One or more members of the O.S.I. made a trip to Lubbock to investigate the incident first-hand, and the photographer was interrogated at length. His account of the incident seemed logical, and there was no obvious indication of a hoax. The photographer had previously been interrogated by the Lubbock newspapers and the photos inspected by the Associated Press and by representatives of *Life* Magazine. It was their opinion that the photos were not obviously a hoax. However, the college professors were doubtful as to whether or not the photographs were of the same objects they had observed, because: (1) They had never observed a V-shaped formation of lights. This is not too significant, however, because the arrangement of the lights that they had observed varied, and since there were several flights, the college professors possibly did not see the flights that were photographed. (2) The lights that the professors observed were, in their opinion, not bright enough to be photographed. This is, however, an estimate, and could be an error.

The Air Technical Intelligence Center at Dayton, Ohio analyzed the photos, and their conclusions were: (1) The images on the negatives were caused by light striking unexposed film, i.e., the negatives were not retouched. (2) The individual lights in the formation varied in intensity. (3) The intensity was greater than any surrounding stars, as the stars did not register. (4) The individual lights changed position in the formation.

The O.S.I. was requested to reinterrogate the photographer in another attempt to determine the authenticity of the photographs. A preliminary report concerning this reinterrogation stated that there was no indication that the photographs were not authentic.

As I retyped the report for my magazine, there seemed to be little doubt that the Lubbock light photos represented the same phenomena that the Texas College professors saw.

But as I carefully proofread the article, twice in fact, as I cogitated, a great deal of doubt began to creep into my mind, and I began to notice a very odd attitude in the Report:

We usually think of the Air Force as subtly or directly trying to discredit genuine sightings and photos, but in this instance we had a most peculiar situation in which the AF was for some strange reason apparently *trying to uphold the authenticity* of pictures which they knew or strongly suspected to be clever fakes.

An unofficial AF admission to this effect, plus my own findings during an on the spot investigation, substantiated my belief that the sighting was genuine but that Hart's photographs were not.

Some of the objections have come directly from one of the professors who had witnessed the sightings.

"You can identify me as *one* of the professors mentioned in the Bluebook report, but please not specifically by name," he told me at his office.

"The things we saw were never in view more than six seconds. For the photographer to have taken the pictures under the conditions we observed would have been impossible."

I had to agree with the professor. In a personal interview with me Hart had told me that the camera exposure he used was very slow—only 1/10 of a second—and other people I saw who had talked to Hart said he had given them the same shutter speed. Yet, even with my inexperience in the field of photography I knew that any fast moving object would produce a blur at that setting.

Yet in only one of the four pictures is there any evidence of blurring and only slightly in that one.

"Suppose that Hart panned the camera," I asked the professor, "moving with the object, to avoid blurring; would that have resulted in a sharp picture?"

"I doubt that 100 per cent," he replied. "I believe I can safely say that no amount of panning could have given him clear photographs of the phenomena we witnessed.

"Further, O.S.I. officers, who investigated our sightings and Hart's photos, told me that his pictures were of lights whose total brilliance would be of several times that of the full moon. Yet the lights we saw were of no such brilliance; in fact these lights were not even bright enough to be photographed at all."

After interviewing two of the other professors, who gave me essentially the same story printed above in the Status report, I talked to many other people in the town, and was further convinced that the photographs were fakes.

In another incident, not involving photographs and a much more serious matter, I was told that Hart stuck to a false, preconceived story in spite of

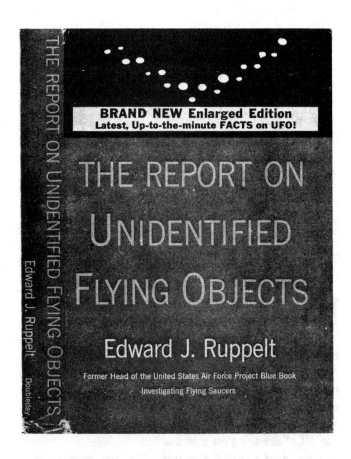

Jacket from Edward J. Ruppelt's book (Doubleday 1956) carries pictures of Lubbock lights.

definite evidence against him. Furthermore, another informant told me that Hart, an ardent amateur photographer, once told him that he would do "anything" to get a picture of his own in a newspaper.

To me it seemed quite evident that the famous Lubbock lights photographs were nothing more than clever fakes that had "taken in" dozens of editors and authors. Taking advantage of the genuine phenomena being seen almost nightly over his home town, Hart apparently found the opportunity he was looking for to achieve a small degree of fame.

But of the phenomena itself, the lights positively could not have been the results of reflections or temperature inversions, nor any of the other popular explanations then in vogue. According to the opinion of the Lubbock professors, they were either a totally unknown unnatural phenomenon, or else one or more solid craft of some sort.

3:15
THE WRIGHT FIELD STORY....
OR "WHO'S LYING?"

Now, technically, by the Ground Rules, Yonah was supposed to be on *my side* on the Long John Show, and to help me castigate Barker, by means of the article by Lonzo Dove in *Saucer News*. But you can't knock Yonah's sense of humor, and I could tell from his quizzical expression that the note he was passing to Long John contained some awful retribution directed to me. "Let me ask you this. . . ."

John was reading the note. "In the apartment house where you live," John continued—and I knew what was coming. John was going to give me a hard time on this, and his face betrayed not one trace of the smile I knew was building deep within him. That, I suppose, is the reason why Long John is the best radio man I know. When you are on the Long John show, he subtly leads the guest--or panelist—into a magic world of belief: in which every word of the Master (L.J.) is imbued with an authority or seriousness.

"How is your name spelled on the building directory?" John continued—and I could see Yonah trying to repress hysterics.

Of course, as Yonah and Long John were forcing me to admit, the name on my apartment house directory was spelled incorrectly, without the "e" in Moseley!

"M-O-S-L-E-Y," John spelled out the name.

Of course, this was supposed to have something to do with the letter Barker had read, which involved the changing of name of "Moseley" to Mosley." I should have appreciated the gag, but somehow when you are on radio, you don't want somebody to be one-up on you, especially Barker that night, since *he* was supposed to be the person *I was "exposing."*

"If you *aren't* in the Air Force," Yonah, still the turncoat, insisted to me, "isn't it strange you can't get a letter from them saying that?"

I launched into the usual complaints of the Average American who writes to the Government and of the Strange Replies he usually receives.

While I was talking I was thinking seriously about the Air Force. About the files I had seen which had been suddenly withdrawn. About the crackpots who claimed the Air Force had little men from flying saucers pickled in formaldyhyde. Then there were, of course, the tales of crashed saucers, and reported scientific examination of them.

When I reviewed such stories of disabled saucers, I always think of my involvement with the Air Force which led me to the most fantastic report I have ever investigated.

And somebody was lying—either the AF or "Miss Y."

The scene had been perfectly set for a weird bit of business. An odd weather condition had added a note of unreality and spectral quality to the Ohio city. It was sunset, and the sky had taken on a frightening red color. Somehow it seemed appropriate, for I had gone to this city to visit an Air Force base where a flying saucer had reportedly crashed. I was locating the base so that I could find it easily the next day.

I planned to find a nearby motel and look for "Miss Y" tomorrow. If my lead had been reliable, she would have a fantastic story to tell.

In looking through the Air Force files I hadn't expected to find, nor found, any reports of captured saucers or little men. Despite official AF denials, however, such rumors still persisted.

The late Frank Scully, well known and highly respected Hollywood writer, had caused a sensation with his book, *Behind the Flying*

Saucers, in which he related how a government scientist had been called in to examine a saucer which had allegedly crashed in New Mexico. Few people now believe Scully's story, which he had obtained from two acquaintances, Silas Newton and Leo Gebauer; for a *True* magazine article had pretty well exposed it as a hoax. It probably wasn't Scully's fault. The article, and other reports suggested that the author had simply been taken in.

But at that time the basic rumor, with many variations, vividly haunted the saucer scene. Every month or so a new crashed saucer report, complete with little men, would appear. Most of these reports came from the southwestern U.S., but there was one from Scandinavia and another from Europe.

I had little faith in the accounts until I bumped into a bizarre investigation of a saucer said to be in the possession of the AF at Wright-Patterson Air Force Base!

Since my perusal of the AF files late in 1953 I had begun corresponding with people all over the U.S. and was becoming fairly well known as a civilian UFO researcher. In April, 1954, one of these correspondents floored me with a letter, from which I quote:

My opinion is that the Air Force is holding a saucer or parts thereof at Wright-Patterson Field. I base this opinion on a great number of collective items—and one solid item, the testimony of a woman who was a WAC at Wright in the fall of 1952 when there was a Red and White aircraft attack alert for two weeks. She learned that a saucer had been brought to Wright Field, and she saw a picture of it!

According to the correspondent, the Air Force had found an operative radio transmitting device inside the machine which regularly gave off "beeps." They were afraid the saucer had signalled for help and might attract other craft and a possible attack. The correspondent believed the saucer had crashed near Columbus, Ohio, but wasn't certain. He also said that bodies of six little men had been found and hauled to the base, along with the machine.

I put down the letter and pulled out my special file on crash rumors. I had dozens of them:

A professor of anthropology at Columbia had supposedly been called out to Wright-Patterson to examine these creatures; a scientist in Massachusetts had made X-rays of the bodies; a man in Los Angeles knew of a saucer that landed in Mexico; a man in Florida had talked to a man who knew of, in turn, a man who had driven a truck for the Army, in which a captured saucer had been carried from the place it had "crashed" to a nearby military base; a doctor in New York had examined bodies of little men in a funeral parlor there...

And so it went. The reports had a great deal in common besides crashed saucers: the people involved were not named, so most of them were uncheckable.

The ones I had been able to check turned out to be hoaxes, or else they had no discoverable factual evidence to back them up. I finally decided that all of the accounts had been appropriated right out of the pages of Scully's book.

So I stuck the letter into the "crash file" to lie with the many unsubstantiated yarns. I would have forgotten it had I not found myself routed through the correspondent's home town about a month later. I decided to stay overnight, got myself a hotel room and rang him up. The man, whom I will call Bill, greeted me enthusiastically on the phone and invited me to his house. From his conversation I gathered he might be the first informant who could provide any real, concrete lead on a captured saucer—for he claimed to have a tape recording of a key informant. For the first time I became really enthusiastic about such a matter. I wished I had not waited so long to follow it up.

When I arrived at Bill's house he already had his recorder set up, and after a preliminary cup of coffee, I began to hear a tape made by a woman who sounded very much as if she really knew what she was talking about!

Immediately impressed by her apparent sincerity, I quickly decided that *here at last was something concrete*—a first-hand account of what a woman working for the government had seen and heard in the course of her duties. Although uncertain about many details (just as many people would be in relating an event which had transpired months before), she in general told her story in such a manner that I could not help feeling that she was probably telling the truth.

There was only one fly in the Ufological ointment. Although the woman's first name (I will refer to her as Miss Y) was on the tape, Bill would not give me her full name, nor tell me how to get in touch with her.

"The fellow who made the recording promised her she would receive absolutely no personal publicity, and made me pledge likewise when he entrusted the tape to my safe keeping. When I wrote you I had no idea that you would take the trouble to come out here and follow it up."

"But Bill," I pressed, "you may be sitting on the hottest news story of all time. Don't you think the public should know about this if it's true?"

"I agree with you, Jim, but a pledge is a pledge. Miss Y is already sorry she made the tape for she fears repercussions should her story leak out."

Miss Y's apparent sincerity on the tape made me determined to smoke her out and talk to her personally for I was convinced that this was one "crash" report really worth following up.

How I finally located Miss Y, three months later, is certainly worth telling, for it is almost like a detective story. But to tell the story I would have to give out many details which most likely would violate the secrecy of the identities of not only her, but others involved; and this I will not do, even at the expense of reader disbelief that these people do really exist. I know this is not good reporting, but if the reader will go along with me in this respect, I will relate what is to me the most fascinating part of this book.

Miss Y turned out to be a rather fragile-looking woman, probably in her late thirties, bespectacled, with her hair neatly done up in a bun. Her entire demeanor was that of meekness, and I think she finally decided to talk with me because she felt sorry for me after my expressions of disappointment.

Now I know that some fragile little old ladies, and middle-aged ones as well, embezzle banks and other employers by the dozens, but I must say that Miss Y seemed to me to be almost the last person in the world who would make up a real whopper—and if Miss Y were lying, she had manufactured a collossal one!

First she straightened me out on some points which Bill had either assumed or got confused. She did not work at Wright-Patterson, but at another large military base in that area which I will not name; she was not a WAC, but rather a civilian employee of the Signal Corps, working under the Army and the FBI (she has since retired and moved away). Her duties, those of a night girl on teletype, included decoding messages and handling classified material of many different sorts. If this were true, I thought, this alone would vouch for her trustworthiness, for such work would require a security clearance granted only after a very thorough check of her background.

In August—or was it September—of 1952 I walked into the photographic lab to get an aspirin from ———, who was in charge of this section (The Army photographer in charge of the lab will be referred to as Mr. Z.). This lab was in the same section of the communication building on the base which I worked in. When I walked in he was developing a number of prints, and I couldn't help noticing that about a dozen of them looked like the newspaper drawings I had seen of flying saucers.

"At first he expressed some concern that I had seen the photos; he thought he had the door locked but had gone to the rest room and forgotten to relock it. Knowing that I had a clearance and being a good friend of mine, he apparently decided to relieve my curiosity."

Mr. Z had personally taken the photos during a recent special assignment at a location Miss Y described simply as "north of the Base." There, according to the technician, a flying saucer had crashed. That in essence was all the information he would give her, as he warned her that the pictures were classified and carried top security designation.

"At the time," Miss Y told me, "I thought this was more or less a routine photographic record of experimental military aircraft which frequently were tested at the base, and thought little more of it until I handled some startling messages.

"The first communications involved information that the aircraft, which was thought to be of interplanetary nature, was being brought first to our Base, under very heavy guard, where it would receive a preliminary examination and then be trucked to Wright Field.

"Further messages ordered a Red and White Alert for the base, since it was feared that the crashed saucer had communicated with other similar craft still flying. This made me very nervous, for it sounded to me as if the base commander believed that other machines might attack in an effort to recover the disabled craft."

Security had been clamped down very tightly. Officers and one scientist were brought in from other bases to complement the staff, and no enlisted men except Mr. Z had anything to do with the matter. No less than a major, Miss Y told me, drove the truck that hauled the craft to the base. Enlisted men were told that the alert was for practice only and that the officers had been flown in to observe how well it was carried out.

"How large do you think the saucer was, from seeing the photographs?" I asked.

"I'm not good at this, but I would say thirty feet in diameter. In a couple or three of the pictures there was a jeep parked by it and this gave a good frame of reference. It would be forty feet at the most, I would say.

"It had no protrusions, other than a rim where the upper and lower halves of the machine met.

"It appeared to be made of pieces of metal riveted together, though I couldn't see any rivets, only the different sections. It didn't have any windows that I could see. Some of the messages, however, mentioned that it had windows or portholes of one-way glass which you couldn't see through from the outside."

Miss Y also said she had heard from Mr. Z that scientists employed by the government had trouble getting inside the saucer, and that it was composed of one or more alloys not found on Earth.

And here her description departed from the classic tale: this saucer contained no dead little men. It was a remotely controlled device, evidently equipped with devices to collect and transmit information. Also, the saucer hadn't really crashed, having floated gently to the ground due to a "lack of magnetic power on which they run."

Miss Y had heard vague information about other saucers which had previously been captured, these actually containing bodies of humanoid creatures. I discounted this part of her story, however, feeling that she had perhaps overheard conversations about the Scully book (she had never read it).

I was still greatly convinced with her sincerity, but I felt I still didn't have quite enough to warrant the conclusion that the Government did actually have a captured saucer and possibly little men.

So I begged Miss Y for the name of Mr. Z, the photographer, which she finally gave me after much hesitation.

"He won't alk, though. I can tell you that right now. He's still on active duty with the Army. He's getting almost ready for retirement and fears anything that might get him discharged."

Whether for the reason that Miss Y gave, or whether she had for some almost unbelievable reason, concocted the story and was indeed lying, she was certainly correct about one thing: Although Mr. Z did talk, it wasn't in confirmation of her account.

He began with a summary denial of having any knowledge of flying saucers, what's more photographing one. During the two-hour conversation, the latter part of which was in the presence of his superior, a Signal Corps officer, he completely refuted her claims.

Miss Y did work as a night girl on teletype during the period she claimed to have been there—but she had never read any highly secret messages. She most likely had handled coded messages, but she had no way of decoding them. If any highly classified messages had indeed come through she would not have known what they contained.

"Sure we know about flying saucers," Mr. Z told me, "but only what we read in the papers. If you run around and investigate these sightings, you know a lot more than we do."

Certainly no saucer had ever passed through their base, and they certainly had no knowledge of saucers captured anywhere by the government—or so they said.

They described Miss Y as a very efficient worker and "an upstanding woman." They couldn't guess why she would be telling such a story.

Walking out of the officer's club, where I interviewed the two, the seemingly almost organized confusion of the saucer mystery began to trouble me. If the two men were telling the truth, Miss Y was *lying*. One thing was obvious: *Somebody was lying*!

As I drove by the rows of barracks to the base exit, I tried to analyze the situation.

First I assumed that Miss Y was telling the truth. She had said that the facts she gave me were "public knowledge" and that she was not breaking security to tell them to me—though on that point I tended to disagree. It was quite understandable that she didn't want her name connected, even though it may have been public knowledge. She also had said that the government was holding back the facts from the public because of fear of panic, and also because they didn't have all the answers yet themselves—these observations probably were only her own personal opinion.

If indeed Miss Y had been telling the truth, it certainly would fit in with Mr. Z's statements. He would be *required* to say she was lying and deny having made the photographs or having knowledge of them.

If the government did indeed have captured saucers, it probably would be known to only a few people, which would include a few with the necessary skills, such as photography, for investigative purposes. Probably none such people would know the full story—only his or her tiny part in the drama. Only a handful of brass at the very top would have all the details, anyhow.

The whole thing would be guarded as well, if not better, than the atomic bomb. If all that Miss Y had told me were true, I doubted if even the people at the Pentagon, whom I had talked with and who had let me see the files, knew it. It was then that I got a fantastic idea. Suppose that the Project Blue Book was merely a cover-up, which analyzed *routine* saucer sightings; while somewhere else, within a highly guarded section of Wright Field—or some other base—a super-secret group was prying open saucers and desperately trying, in an attempt to get ahead of the Russians, to find out what made them and their extraterrestrial operators tick!

In keeping these secrers, the government had many advantages, and the main one probably was that the saucers themselves carried a ridiculous connotation in the minds of most of the public. Quite possibly, of course, there were very effective ways of dealing with individuals, in or out of the service, who knew too much or and talked too much.

In Scully's case (if his story had some truth to it) it was fairly simple: he was not dealt with in any dire cloak-and-dagger manner, but by the simple technique of *ridicule.* At first his book caused a sensation; now very few people believe it, for every possible effort has apparently been made to discredit and make him look ridiculous. Two principal characters of the book had been arrested on fraud charges, and they, their cases then undisposed of, were claiming that they were being persecuted for their saucer revelations. Could they be right and could Miss Y be right? There probably was a fifty-fifty choice either way.

I thought of the flying saucer the Canadian Government had first started building and later sold to the U.S. Department of Defense. Were we desperately trying to build such a machine, basing our design on what we had learned from the possible inspection of genuine interplanetary craft? True, the news releases said the AVRO Saucer would employ conventional jet power. (*Later the government put the AVRO saucer on public display and indicated its design was unsuccessful. But its design would be strangely changed from that of the much publicized jet craft and turn out to be a ducted-fan hovercraft much like the model the British experimented with about the same time.* Was the AVRO saucer a red herring or a possible preparation of the public to accept some startling announcements and increased congressional appropriations?

If saucers were real, they certainly didn't run on jet power. Many technicians had suggested that they must employ control of gravity and likely involve an electromagnetic drive. If the government had indeed captured a saucer or saucers it certainly appeared likely that they could unravel the power secrets involved.

When *would* the public be informed about the entire matter? Probably only when the government was good and ready, and only after they had mastered the secrets of the captured discs and learned from their operators the purpose of the visits. We would probably be told only after years of being gradually prepared and indoctrinated. This could be done in many ways, with more red herrings, such as George Adamski; with carefully conceived reports such as the AVRO saucer.

I wondered if the public should know *sooner.* After all, I was part of the public, and I didn't think I would panic if I suddenly knew the saucers were real. And I was becoming convinced, more and more each day, that they certainly *weren't* temperature inversions and all the other things the government said they were.

Yes, *somebody was lying.* If Miss Y were lying, there wasn't anything to the captured saucer. Yet if Miss Y were *not* lying, somebody should be able to prove it and somebody should tell the public.

If Miss Y were *not* lying, Mr. Z *would have to lie!*

What could I do about it? Not much for I probably exaggerated my own effectiveness.

But there was one way I could raise a lot of hell in the field, and probably get a lot of public awareness going. Albert Bender had done it and lately Gray Barker was arousing a lot of public interest with his *Saucerian.*

Knowing very little about how to do it, and with a bravado effected, it seems, only by brash people who have been hooked on saucers, I headed my Ford back toward Fort Lee, New Jersey.

If I drove hard I could make it back home sometime in the early hours of the next morning. I doubted if I would even go to bed. For the next day *I would start my own flying saucer magazine.*

3:25
DR. D'S STRANGE THEORY

As I referred again to my exposé article in *Saucer News*, and Gray Barker further defended himself on the Long John Show, I noted the difference between the neatly-printed offset publication as it was now, and the old *Nexus* I began publishing after returning from Ohio.

The first issues of *Nexus*, were cranked out on an old mimeograph machine. Physically, its publication was as simple as typing the material out on a stencil and then helping August C. Roberts, whom I named associate editor, turn the crank.

I wondered which version. I really liked the best—the old crudely-printed issues or the slick new ones I had passed out to the Long John panel.

It was in the *Nexus* days when I first ran into the Earth Theory. I sometimes regret that I ever got started on the "Theory" at all, for it alienated popular support for my magazine and made me disliked among many segments of saucerdom.

But I had a lead and I wanted to check it out. And the best way to check out a theory is to publish information about it and seek public reaction.

It all began when I picked up the phone and rang up Leonard Stringfield, a prominent UFO civilian researcher of Cincinnati. I thought I'd pass the time of day, compare notes, and ask him for some ideas.

"I have just received a letter from a fellow you ought to meet," Len told me. "A scientist who lives in New York State. I'll give you his name but I warn you, agree to refer to him only by his pseudonym, Dr. D., or you'll get very little information out of him."

"What gives with him?" I queried.

"His theories on saucers are ridiculous—but you know I'm an interplanetary buff from A to Z. He

thinks the saucers come from Earth, are built by the U.S. Government. It may not be too popular with your readers, but it would be interesting if you interviewed him or had him do an article for you. He seems to be very cooperative with the UFO press. Personally I think his theories can't hold up—you know, saucers are nothing new and have been flying around since the dawn of recorded history.

"What really interests me about "Dr. D.' is . . . . ."

There were some noises on the line and Len paused.

"Well, make up your own mind on him. The most I can say over the phone is that I think you'll find it interesting if you read between the lines of everything he tells you."

Then he gave me Dr. D.'s name and address and I promised to drop by Cincinnati as soon as possible and see Len personally. Although I frequently heard the usual noises on the telephone, I really hoped the Silence Group, if indeed there was one, was actually listening. In phone conversations I had the habit of kidding whoever *might* be listening. While Len and some of the other saucerers seemed to fear being wire tapped, I would usually throw them some whoppers, especially while talking with close friends who were "in" on my own little bit of paranoia. I usually announced that I was planning to assassinate the president of Brazil, or that I had a secret informant in the Pentagon who had given me classified Bomb secrets. This, I figured, would provide anybody *really* listening in something to check on for a few weeks. Then I always gave names of my imaginary accomplices, specific dates and so on.

After I had hung up with Len I put a long

distance call through to this man, whom I will dutifully refer to as Dr. D.

"Oh yes, Jim," he said. "I've been thinking of calling you but haven't got around to it. Say, I've enjoyed your magazine very much." (I wondered how he had read the magazine since I had the small mailing list almost memorized and he wasn't on it—nor was it on the newsstands.)

Dr. D. said he would be very happy to grant me an interview, and that he had many things to discuss which he would rather not go into over the phone. Yes, if I drove up that very night, he would be glad to see me.

"My wife and I were thinking of going out tonight, then I caught this cold. If you aren't afraid of catching it, drive on out. We'll probably have something to eat .about 7:00; why not start early enough and join us at dinner? Nothing fancy, but you're welcome."

Dr. D. turned out to be a very affable man in his late thirties with a very fine sense of humor. Although he began by calling many of the civilian researchers "big nuts" (much to his wife's censure), I could tell he was deeply interested in the subject.

"Now there's some of this stuff (the saucers) that I can't figure out. But my background and certain information at my disposal should qualify me to explain at least some of it. The Adamski bit and some of the other contactees is a bit more difficult, but I think I have a line on them too. Still there are a few sightings that just don't fit into the information I have."

Dr. D. then gave me a persuasive argument that saucers are made on Earth.

"First let me assure you that if it were permissible I could show you some photographs and documents which would be very convincing. You can publish anything I say and later I may write an article or so for you if you wish. What I have to say is in no way classified because I do not have this particular information in documented form and speak only as a private citizen."

I was all ears.

"As you know, the Army and the Army Air Force were made two separate entities in 1947. This still didn't help the interservice revalries, for the old feud between the Navy and the Army was merely carried over into the Air Force itself. This the general public may not be aware of, except for occasional outbursts such as the Navy fight against the B-35, the Air Force fight against the Forrestal-class supercarriers and so on.

"Those who read the aviation and military journals and follow the Washington news reports closely, accept the continuing Navy-Air Force fight as one of the facts of American political life.

"I claim that no one can understand the flying saucer situation without a good knowledge of this grudge."

Dr. D. paused, and rather impishly asked me if I knew that the AF had secretly changed the name of its saucer investigation to Project Grudge early in 1949. I had heard about it, though had ascribed no particular significance to it.

"Prior to 1952 the Air Force denied, not only that the saucers were interplanetary, but U.S. made as well. If you'll think back however, Jim, I don't think you can come up with any official *Navy* statements to the effect that they were *not* made on earth."

I tried to recall any such statements, but couldn't. Come to think of it, the Navy had been very quiet on the subject.

"The year 1947, when the sightings first commenced on any big scale, has another significance as being just prior to the 'unification' of the U.S. Armed Forces. The interservice rivalry between the Army and Navy, and between each of these and the Air Force, is well known, and still exists. This rivalry would have assured that the Air Force would have been kept uninformed of secret aviation developments by the Navy in 1947. It is documented in the Project Grudge report that it was in early 1949 (after unification had got well started) that an Air Force general instructed the flying saucer investigators to change the project code name from Sign to Grudge, to stop spending money on special investigations and to wind up the project during 1949. To me, this indicates that the general had at last been informed of the Navy's developments, and was stopping the ridiculous investigation of our own devices. Prior to unification, the Navy had felt that it was perfectly fair to let the Air Force try to find out for itself what the saucers really were.

"To be brief, the Air Force found out that the Navy had saucer-shaped craft in 1952, and that was the year that General Samford came out with his somewhat befuddling but widely publicized statements that saucers were not extraterrestial."

I checked some newspaper clippings and transcripts Dr. D. handed me describing and quoting the conference. One reporter had asked General Samford if the saucers were "some very highly secret new weapon that we're working on." Samford evaded the question the first time, but the second time he gave as his answer a very definite but misleading statement: "We have nothing that

> Mr. ████ also discussed this matter with Colonel L. R. Forney of MID. Colonel Forney indicated that it was his attitude that inasmuch as it has been established that the flying disks are not the result of any Army or Navy experiments, the matter is of interest to the FBI. He stated that he was of the opinion that the Bureau, if at all possible, should accede to General Schulgen's request.

7-15

(J. Edgar Hoover)

I would do it but before agreeing to it we must insist upon full access to discs recovered. For instance in the La. case the Army grabbed it & would not let us have it for cursory examination.

- 3 -

H.

Memo from FBI agent Ladd and handwritten reply from FBI Director J. Edgar Hoover regarding recovery of crashed disc.

has no mass and unlimited power!"

"That statement," said Dr. D., pointing to the clipping," as anybody with a high school education knows, is a definite evasion of the question, not an answer not a denial, *since every real object must have some mass.*

"To sum up, the Air Force has a 98 per cent assurance that the saucers are Navy made. They will not say this because of the security involved and the fear of giving credit to their arch rival. Then Project Bluebook, understaffed and a sort of Siberia, it often seems, for Air Force officers, may not really know what is going on. They still have to run out, chasing the saucer stories, probably in the dark as to what those at the top really know."

"You mentioned Adamski," I reminded Dr. D. "There may be nothing to his story, but the UFO field is flooded with contactees these days. I frankly don't believe these yarns but I haven't discounted them entirely. I sort of think that where there's fiery-eyed saucer zealots, there just may be some saucers to be smoked out."

"I haven't made a study of the other contactees, for the information wasn't readily available to me," Dr. D. continued, lighting his pipe in which he had put some aromatic tobacco.

"I'm a poor man, but if I weren't I'd lay money on Adamski. But I'm still not laying money that he contacted a long-haired Venusian."

"Whom did he contact then?"

"Probably the CIA, though there are other agencies. There was an elaborate setup. George was taken inside a mock-up flying saucer which didn't actually fly. You've seen Cinerama and how it looks so real. Take a gooked-up saucer and a little hypnotism to a man who wants to believe in it anyhow and even a 16 mm. projector on a screen through some portholes, and you have a real tour to Mars, Venus, or even Perth Amboy, depending upon where they want you to think you went!"

"But the CIA isn't interested in collecting the royalties from Adamski's books—he's in for all the dough," I protested. "Now I don't believe Adamski, but what you're telling me is more fantastic than his story."

Then Dr. D. launched into an elaborate framework which he thought explained the role and motives of the CIA. Though not very convincing to me, I don't think I should publish the material, just in case the theory is valid. Suffice it to say that the theory involved the cold war and U.S. relationships with the Soviet Union.

I drove back to New Jersey not a little dazed by Dr. D's theories. I had asked him to write some articles for *Nexus* outlining his strange views, and for several years these would appear. I remember thinking that his theories, while they sounded logical at the moment, were just a little too pat. Also, they could not account for the historical sightings. But there seemed too much of a possibility of truth in what he had told me to completely discount his statements.

3:30
THE TWELVE BEST SAUCERS

Later I was even more puzzled about Dr. D.'s role in the flying saucer drama.

On May 5, 1955, the Air Force released a controversial document to the public. With the excuse that the reproduction costs of the document for any wide public distribution was prohibitive, the AF made the report available only to people who took the trouble to visit the Information Offices in the Pentagon, New York and Los Angeles.

But the lengthy document, running more than 75 pages, did not prove too expensive for Dr. D., a private individual without apparent wealth, to reproduce and distribute widely! The print job that the AF, with millions at its command, could not allegedly afford, *Dr. D. managed to finance!*

He promoted and distributed it widely, its modest price tag obviously only a part of its actual per copy cost.

To the average individual with only a surface interest in the UFO enigma, *Project Blue Book Special Report No. 14* was a time-consuming bore, which, by the employment of elaborate graphs and statistical gobblegook, purported to prove that only a small percentage of reported sightings (3 per cent or less) remained unexplained.

When I heard that Dr. D. had reproduced the document, I dutifully sent my check for $1.50 and in due course had a copy in my hands. Paper-wise, it certainly was worth the money, but the graphs and statistics I found quite taxing.

The civilian publisher had seen fit to follow both the then current AF line and provide a dramatic cover illustration. The stiff paper cover (appropriately, blue) carried the current artist's conception of the flying saucer the Department of Defense was building—the famous AVRO saucer discussed above.

The illustration, widely carried by the press, suggested that the flying saucers Joe Doakes was seeing probably involved an already-developed device comfortably in the possession of the United States Government.

Later the AF would admit that the AVRO saucer, though it cost a lot of dough, actually failed to fly. Rumor had it that the test pilot who tried to get it off the ground almost got killed in the process, when the U.S. saucer, unlike the alleged interplanetary ones, took a nose dive like Darius Green's Wonderful Machine.

Report No. 14, however, displayed a characteristic ambivalence the AF often let sneak into their official pronouncements. If it figuratively swore on a stack of statistics that flying saucers were the bunk, it nevertheless always left itself a loophole by admitting that a small percentage of sightings submitted were unexplained, or involved "unknowns," as the apparently honest-to-goodness saucers are termed by the AF.

So the literary saving grace of *Report No. 14* consisted of what the AF termed the "Twelve Best Sightings"—terrestrials' encounters with saucers which were the most difficult—or impossible—to explain. The twelve sightings were accompanied by some dramatic drawings which would tend to put some of the wildest UFO books to shame. We reproduce both the text and the drawings in the following pages:

Case I (Serial 0573.00)

Two men employed by a rug-cleaning firm were driving across a bridge at 0955 hours on July 29, 1948, when they saw an object glide across the road a few hundred feet in front of them. It was shiny and metallic in construction, about 6 to 8 feet long and 2 feet wide. It was in a flat glide path at an altitude of about 30 feet and in a moderate turn to the left. It was seen for only a few seconds and apparently went down in a wooded area, although no trace of it was found.

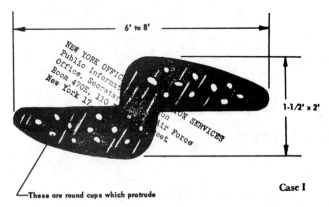

These are round cups which protrude

Case I

Case II (Serial 4508.00)

A naval aviation student, his wife, and several others were at a drive-in movie from 2115 to 2240 hours on April 20, 1952, during which time they saw several groups of objects fly over. There were from two to nine objects in a group and there were about 20 groups. The groups of objects flew in a straight line except for some changes in direction accomplished in a manner like any standard aircraft turn.

The objects were shaped like conventional aircraft. The unaccountable feature of the objects was that each had a red glow surrounding it and was glowing itself, although it was a cloudless night.

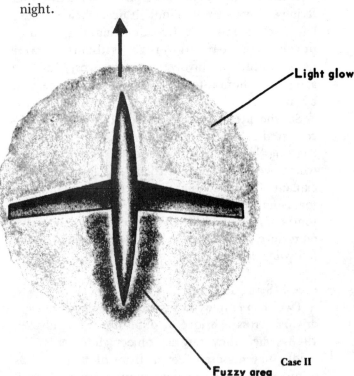

Light glow

Fuzzy area

Case II

Case III (Serial 2013.00, 2014.00, and 2014.01)

Two tower operators sighted a light over a city airport at 2020 hours on January 20, 1951. Since a commercial plane was taking off at this time, the pilots were asked to investigate this light. They observed it at 2026 hours. According to them, it flew abreast of them at a greater radius as they made their climbing turn, during which time it blinked some lights which looked like running lights. While the observing plane was still in its climbing turn, the object made a turn toward the plane and flew across its nose. As the two men turned their heads to watch it, it instantly appeared on their other side flying in the same direction as they were flying, and then in 2 or 3 seconds it slipped under them, and they did not see it again. Total time of the observation was not stated. In appearance, it was like an airplane with a cigar-shaped body and straight wings, somewhat larger than a B-29. No engine nacelles were observed on the wings.

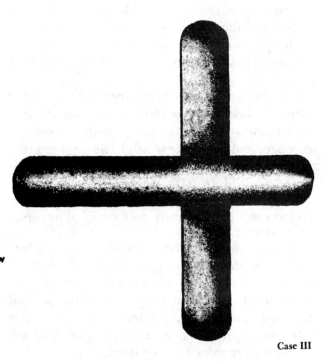

Case III

Case IV (Serial 4599.00)

A part-time farmer and a hired hand were curing tobacco at midnight on July 19, 1952, when they looked up and saw two cigar-shaped objects. One hovered while the other moved to the east and came back, at which time both ascended until out of sight. Duration of observation was 3 to 4 minutes. Both had an exhaust at one end, and neither had projections of any kind. It was stated that they appeared to be transparent and illuminated from the inside.

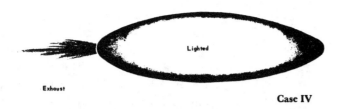

Lighted

Exhaust

Case IV

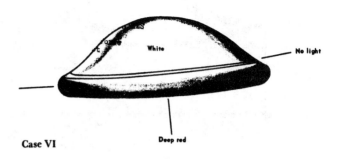

White

No light

Case VI

Deep red

Case V (Serial 0565.00 to 0565.03)

A pilot and copilot were flying a DC-3 at 0340 hours on July 24, 1948, when they saw an object coming toward them. It passed to the right and slightly above them, at which time it went into a steep climb and was lost from sight in some clouds. Duration of the observation was about 10 seconds. One passenger was able to catch a flash of light as the object passed. The object seemed powered by rocket or jet motors shooting a trail of fire some 50 feet to the rear of the object. The object had no wings or other protrusion and had two rows of lighted windows.

Case VII (Serial 2728.00)

A Flight Sergeant saw an object over an Air Force base in Korea at 0842 hours on June 6, 1952. The object flew in a series of spinning and tumbling actions. It was on an erratic course, first flying level, then stopping momentarily, shooting straight up, flying level and again tumbling, then changing course and disappearing into the sun. It reappeared and was seen flying back and forth across the sun. At one time an F-86 passed between the observer and the object. He pointed it out to another man who saw it as it maneuvered near the sun.

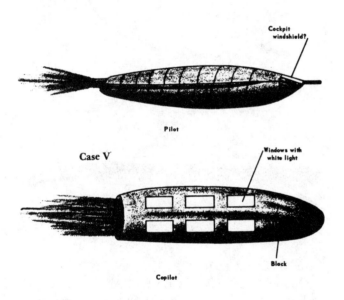

Cockpit windshield?

Pilot

Case V

Windows with white light

Black

Copilot

Case VI (Serial 4822.00)

An instrument technician, while driving from a large city toward an Air Force base on December 22, 1952, saw an object from his car at 1930 hours. He stopped his car to watch it. It suddenly moved up toward the zenith in spurts from right to left at an angle of about 45 degrees. It then moved off in level flight at a high rate of speed, during which maneuver it appeared white most of the time, but apparently rolled three times showing a red side. About halfway through its roll it showed no light at all. It finally assumed a position to the south of the planet Jupiter at a high altitude, at which position it darted back and forth, left and right alternately. Total time of the observation was

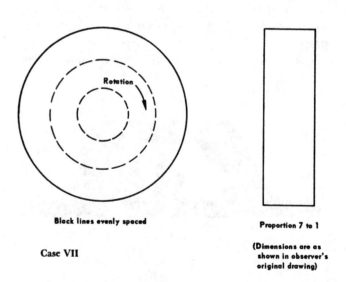

Rotation

Black lines evenly spaced

Case VII

Proportion 7 to 1

(Dimensions are as shown in observer's original drawing)

Case VIII (Serial 0576.00)

An electrician was standing by the bathroom window of his home, facing west, at 0825 hours on July 31, 1948, when he first sighted an object. He ran to his kitchen where he pointed out the object to his wife. Total time in sight was approximately 10 seconds, during which the object flew on a straight and level course from horizon to horizon, west to east.

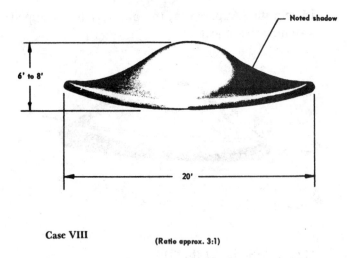

6' to 8'

20'

Noted shadow

Case VIII

(Ratio approx. 3:1)

Case IX (Serial 0066.00)

A farmer and his two sons, aged 8 and 10, were at his fishing camp on August 13, 1947. At about 1300 hours, he went to look for the boys, having sent them to the river for some tape from his boat. He noticed an object some 300 feet away, 75 feet above the ground. He saw it against the background of the canyon wall which was 400 feet high at this point. It was hedge hopping, following the contour of the ground, was sky blue, about 20 feet in diameter and 10 feet thick, and had pods on the side from which flames were shooting out. It made a swishing sound. The observer stated that the trees were highly agitated by the craft as it passed over. His two sons also observed the object. No one saw the object for more than a few seconds.

Side view

Case IX

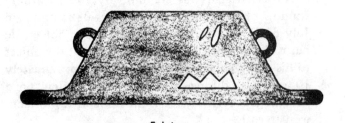

End view

Case X (Serial 1119.00)

An employee in the supersonic laboratory of an aeronautical laboratory and some other employees of this lab, were by a river, 2½ miles from its mouth, when they saw an object. The time was about 1700 hours on May 24, 1949. The object was reflecting sunlight when observed by naked eye. However, he then looked at it with 8-power binoculars, at which time there was no glare. (Did glasses have filter?) It was of metallic construction and was seen with good enough resolution to show that the skin was dirty. It moved off in horizontal flight at a gradually increasing rate of speed, until it seemed to approach the speed of a jet before it disappeared. No propulsion was apparent. Time of observation was 2½ to 3 minutes.

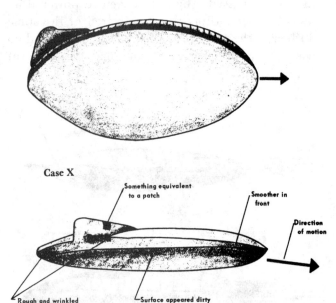

Case X

Something equivalent to a patch

Smoother in front

Direction of motion

Rough and wrinkled in rear

Surface appeared dirty and spotty in color

Direction of motion

Case XI (Serial 1550.00)

On March 20, 1950, a Reserve Air Force Captain and an airlines Captain were flying a commercial airlines flight. At 21:26, the airline Captain directed the attention of the Reserve Air Force Captain to an object which apparently was flying at high speed, approaching the airliner from the south on a north heading. The Reserve Air Force Captain focused his attention on the object. Both crew members watched it as it passed in front of them and went out of sight to the right. The observation, which lasted about 25 to 35 seconds, occurred about 15 miles north of a medium-sized city. When the object passed in front of the airliner, it was not more than ½ mile distant and at an altitude of about 1000 feet higher than the airliner.

The object appeared to be circular, with a

diameter of approximately 100 feet and with a vertical height considerably less than the diameter, giving the object a disc-like shape. In the top center was a light which was blinking at an estimated 3 flashes per second. This light was so brilliant that it would have been impossible to look at it continuously had it not been blinking. This light could be seen only when the object was approaching and after it had passed the airliner. When the object passed in front of the observers, the bottom side was visible. The bottom side appeared to have 9 to 12 symmetrical oval or circular portholes located in a circle approximately 3/4 of the distance from the center to the outer edge. Through these portholes came a soft purple light about the shade of aircraft fluorescent lights. The object was traveling in a straight line without spinning. Considering the visibility, the length of time the object was in sight, and the distance from the object, the Reserve Air Force Captain estimates the speed to be in excess of 1000 mph.

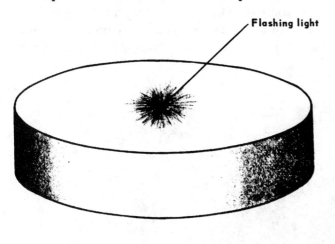

Case XI

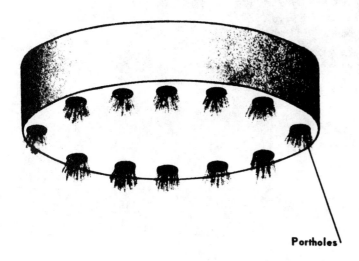

Portholes

Case XII (Serial 3601.00)

At 0535 on the morning of August 25, 1952, a musician for a radio station was driving to work from his home when he noticed an object hovering about 10 feet above a field near the road along which he was driving. As he came abreast of the object, he stopped his car and got out to watch. Having an artificial leg, he could not leave the road, since the surrounding terrain was rough. However, he was within about 100 yards of it at the point he was standing on the road. The object was not absolutely still, but seemed to rock slightly as it hovered. When he turned off the motor of his car, he could hear a deep throbbing sound coming from the object. As he got out of the car, the object began a vertical ascent with a sound similar to "a large covey of quail starting to fly at one time". The object ascended vertically through broken clouds until out of sight. His view was not obscured by clouds. The observer states that the vegetation was blown about by the object when it was near the ground.

Description of the object is as follows:

It was about 75 feet long, 45 feet wide, and 15 feet thick, shaped like two oval meat platters placed together. It was a dull aluminum color, and had a smooth surface. A medium-blue continuous light shone through the one window in the front section. The head and shoulders of one man, sitting motionless, facing the forward edge of the object, were visible. In the midsection of the object were several windows extending from the top to the rear edge of the object; the midsection of the ship had a blue light which gradually changed to different shades. There was a large amount of activity and movement in the midsection that could not be identified as either human or mechanical, although it did not have a regular pattern of movement. There were no windows, doors or portholes, vents, seams, etc., visible to the observer in the rear section of the object or under the object (viewed at time of ascent). Another identifiable feature was a series of propellers 6 to 12 inches in diameter spaced closely together along the outer edge of the object. These propellers were mounted on a bracket so that they revolved in a horizontal plane along the edge of the object. The propellers were revolving at a high rate of speed.

Investigation of the area soon afterward showed some evidence of vegetation being blown around. An examination of grass and soil samples taken indicated nothing unusual. Reliability of the observer was considered good.

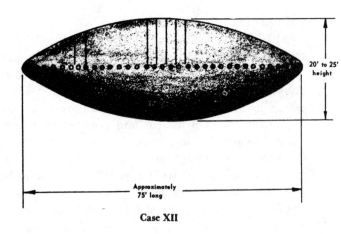

20' to 25' height

Approximately 75' long

Case XII

Dr. D. would continue to be a puzzling personality in the UFO investigation field.

For a while he dropped out of active research, only to show up again at a party given in New York in the honor of Al K. Bender, finally coaxed from his Bridgeport, Conn., home to make a short appearance on the Long John Show.

"Dr. D. did a real peculiar thing," Al told me after drawing me aside.

"So you think he's mysterious too," I half kidded Al.

"He asked permission to take my picture with his Polaroid, and of course that was all right," Al said. "But then he asked me to get up and stand aside while he took a picture of the empty chair. Then he sat me down again and snapped the picture. The picture of the empty chair and then me in it turned out fine. He even made an extra print for me."

"Did he explain the empty chair bit?" I asked.

"Only that it was what he termed 'a control shot,'" Al replied.

I doubt very much if Dr. D. was or is a member of the Silence Group, and I doubt very much that I will ever *completely* believe he isn't.

A couple of years later Dr. D. ran out of copies of *Project Blue Book Special Report No. 14*. Whatever the merits of this special Air Force report, it must have a special place in the heart of Dr. D. (Through special permission of Dr. D., a new expanded edition of *Project Blue Book Special Report No. 14* is now available from Saucerian Books [Box 2228, Clarksburg, W. Va.] at $5.95. This limited edition contains much additional documentation by Dr. D., and consists of more than 100 large 8½ x 11" pages. It is available at $5.95.)

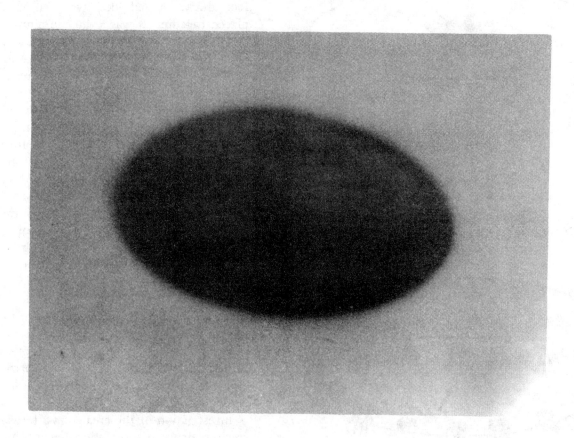

"I think I know what Ray Palmer's *fact* is," Yonah averred.

All of us on the Long John Show turned and looked at him, mouths wide open. For we'd all read Palmer's many statements and had often kicked this around in bull sessions.

Tonight it had come up again and we were wondering if Palmer really knew some fact which enabled him, as he claimed, to know whether a given account about flying saucers, contactees, and so on was true or false.

Where Palmer had got the fact, nobody knew—if indeed he had one. For Palmer always stopped there. If he revealed the "fact," it would invalidate his use of it, for people might deliberately fabricate yarns to conform with it.

"Ray Palmer invented flying saucers!" Yonah continued. "He knows there is nothing to them since he made them up in the first place!"

True, Palmer had publicized Kenneth Arnold's famous 1947 sighting, the first one to gain any publicity, in *Fate* magazine and in a book co-authored by Arnold titled *The Coming of the Saucers*.

I wish Ed had Ray's "fact"—if indeed there were any such thing! It might help me evaluate one of the strangest experiences I have encountered while involved with saucer research.

As each year goes by, my suspicions grow. And those suspicions are that I was hoaxed. As time goes by, and I reflect on it, the whole thing just doesn't make sense. If I *were* hoaxed, the hoaxter must have had sick and complex motives.

I wonder if Bender, the subject of most of the discussion that evening, might have had some similar experience. I didn't really think that Gray Barker had hired the three men in black to visit and frighten Bender, but the subject we were discussing did, come to think of it, contain some similar content.

About a week after I had talked with Dr. D., a knock came at my door.

"Are you the James Moseley who publishes the flying saucer magazine?" a young man, probably in his thirties, asked. The man, about five feet nine and just beginning to bald, was dressed in a gray, Madison Avenue suit, and employed some of the mannerisms and vocabulary of that establishment.

I decided to invite him in, for he did not seem to be the usual type of saucer fan who came to my place to ask me questions (which I always enjoyed answering) but who usually harrangued me for an inordinate period of time about the flying saucer he had seen, and his own private theories.

It developed, however, that the man was after all like such fans in one respect. He didn't want to find out anything, but he did want to tell me many things.

"Look," I told him, "I'm very busy. I have these stencils almost typed for my next issue and have to put in three or four more paragraphs and proof read the thing in order to 'get it to bed.' "

While I was thus remonstrating the man was unzipping a neat leather portfolio, and he then withdrew about seven photographs from it and tossed them on the coffee table between us.

I must have sounded like a phonograph running d o w n. "A r e . . . . . y o u . . . submitting. . .these. . .for. . .publication?"

"You might say that. All seven of these can be published in your. . .what is it, *Nexus*, all for the sum of. . .well, let's be reasonable and settle for a couple of beers."

This guy had the most tremendous saucer photographs I have ever seen. Real close up stuff.

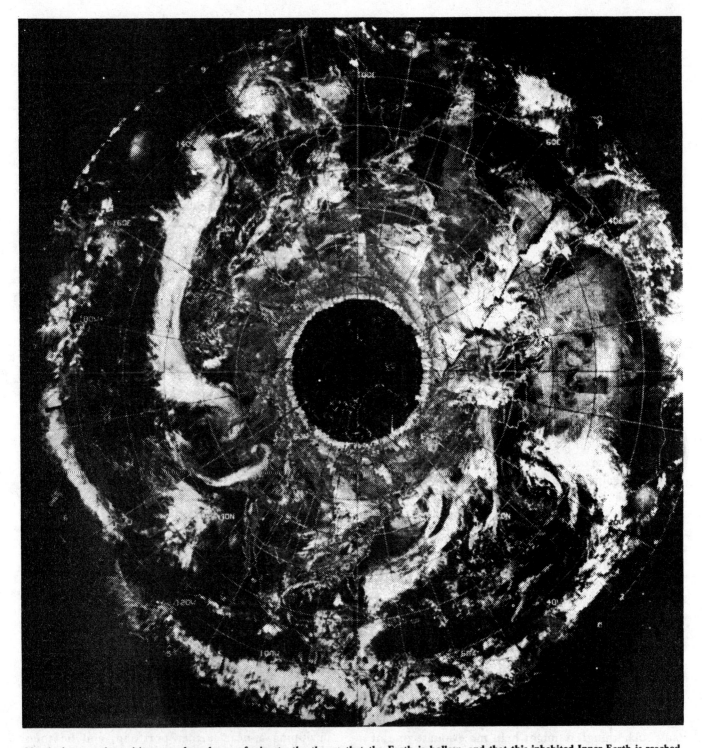

Moseley's mysterious visitor may have been referring to the theory that the Earth is hollow, and that this inhabited Inner Earth is reached through openings at the poles. This ESSA-7 Satellite photo of the North Pole clearly shows a dark circular area. Our thanks to Ray Palmer, editor of FLYING SAUCERS magazine (Palmer Publications, Box AD, Amherst, Wisconsin) for use of this photograph.

Saucers, yes, but unlike the ones I had seen. Portholes, doors, antenna, and even markings in unfamiliar symbols. I can't remember the details now, but I do recall that one of them was very much like a photo Gray Barker had published in his *Saucerian*. It had a large "tail rudder," or "handle," and I had kidded him that it looked like a flying cup. Barker claimed it had been found in the reject bin of a color lab that did secret work for the Air Force.

The man's photos were not black and white, but had a reddish, sepia-like quality. In fact they reminded me of the proofs I had received of my high school graduation pictures.

"They're all yours, Jim—that is, if you can publish them in the next hour before they fade. Soon you'll have seven nice big eight by ten pieces of black photographic paper. I'm going to talk to you about five minutes longer than that," the man, still friendly, but now with an almost cynical touch, announced.

Then I remembered how the photographer had made several graduation photos of me and gave these to my mother. The prints, however, had not been "fixed" with hypo and soon faded out after we had selected the particular pose we wanted the prints and enlargements made from.

"Just who are you, pal?" I asked him.

"I represent the F.P.S.—that's the Free Photo Service. To you at least Jim. That is with just one condition. You have just seen seven samples. I could have brought you six or eight or nine, or any reasonable quantity; but somehow seven seems to be a mystical number you fanatics go for."

"Are these photos fakes?"

"Take them to any photo expert in the country," was his evasive reply. "Only get them there quick before they fade."

I wondered what the man's game was. I didn't think he was a nut, for he approached me in such a cynical non-nut fashion which was completely disarming.

But suddenly he became more serious.

"Jim," he said, "I have a real story for you to publish—just the way I tell it to you and no other way. And do you know what my safeguards on this are?"

"I think I do," I replied, "and I'll bite."

I thumbed once more through the photos, even then having turned noticably darker.

"O.K. You get the photos and I give you something to go with them."

I asked him to explain the conditions.

"I'll deliver these photos in time for your November issue. Only they will be real photo prints and won't fade out when the light strikes them.

"Write the article based on the material I'm about to give you and put it under a pseudonym, such as Fred Broman, or Richard Cohen, or other names you have used for your own articles.

"By the way, what is your name?"

"I'd 'like for you to call me Bob," was the way he evaded that question.

"All right, when can I have the real photos?"

"I will contact you again in two weeks. Show me the finished article and if it's accurate you may have the photos to back you up."

"What if it isn't accurate?"

"I'll ask you to rewrite or not to publish the article."

"What could you do if I misquoted you and insisted on publishing it," I asked, subtly suggesting that he might be a government agent.

"You don't look like the type who would go back on his word," again came the evasive answer.

I wondered if there could be any pitfalls in listening to what he had to say.

"You aren't going to tell me something about UFOs and place me under security are you?"

"Don't be ridiculous. How could I do that?"

Bob indicated he was ready to give me his information.

"Now if you'll get out lots of notepaper, I'll talk to you exactly one hour. If I go too fast, tell me and I'll slow down."

I got the notepaper, an extra pack of cigarettes and noticed that I had a half-filled bottle of Scotch. I asked from the kitchen if he'd like a drink, and he accepted. I brought him some ice and a mixer, deciding not to have any myself, for I very seldom drink.

"First," he began, "let me qualify somewhat the information I am about to give you. Some flying saucers may come here from some far galaxy, but then once, say, in a thousand years or longer. The only planet in our solar system where saucers might originate is Mars, but that's extremely unlikely. The flying saucers, the ones you're currently hearing the reports about and possibly have seen yourself, are coming from right here on this planet, known to us Earthmen as Earth."

I put down my pad, and was ready to remonstrate when Bob interjected with "Uh!-Uh!-Uh!—just a minute, Jim."

He told me I was going to say this wouldn't explain the historical sightings.

"Did I say they are made by *our* government? Or some other *known* government? Of course not."

This guy was a real wild one. Next, he'll probably tell me that they came from the South Pole!

"Jim, the flying saucers are manufactured and based in the vicinity of Antarctica!"

I had heard from Roberts and Lucchesi that Al Bender had been exploring an Antarctica theory before he had been hushed up by the alleged three men in black. He had been working with Harold H. Fulton, of Australia, on this, though neither had reached any conclusions.

"Let's start with a little background," Bob said,

and drew a folder from his portfolio. He did not offer to show me the document.

"It seems that in many investigations of UFOs by teams of qualified scientists, it has been established that the background radiation content of the atmosphere increased sharply on several occasions at the same time a flying saucer was observed visually in the vicinity of the radiation measuring equipment.

"The report I have here continues and says that this proof was not sufficient to reach any conclusions because no photographs were ever taken of any of the saucers seen visually when the radiation count on the instruments increased."

"I don't see why a photo would be needed for proof," I interjected.

"I don't either," he replied, "unless these scientists didn't trust peoples' eyesight."

"Anyhow," he continued, "the radiation clue mentioned here *is* correct. Some people in the government know this, but not necessarily the air force. Sure the people at the very top all know this, but they don't deal directly with it in the investigations which are still being carried out. I'm not talking of a government agency you would know about—nor the air force, nor the other services.

"For convenience, I'll just refer to it from here on as The Organization.

"Interplanetary saucers, if there be such and *our* group has nothing to do with them, does not concern The Organization. The type The Organization does not want us to know about operate on atomic energy. They employ a means of converting atomic radiation into electrical energy, and they operate by means of this combination—which, of course, represents an entirely new and previously unknown type of propulsion. These machines vary in size from about two to thirty feet in diameter. And there aren't any little green men in them—they are remotely controlled. That's why they can perform the so-called impossible maneuvers which would kill a pilot with the G-forces involved.

"What I'm going to tell you next is not *the* big secret, but it has to be dealt with carefully because it is a part of *the* big secret."

"Why," I interjected, "is it a big secret—fear of panic as is often claimed?"

"Yes and no. And politics. A test was recently run in a small town wherein the residents were led to believe that flying saucers were real and were, as I recall, from some mythical unknown planet hidden behind the moon. The citizens were fearful, all right, but not overly-alarmed. A poll taken by evaluaters proved, for one thing, that their politics had become more conservatively oriented, and surveys showed more ordering of flying saucer literature from the occult book distributors. The people did some minor hoarding. You won't believe this but many people set up souvenir stands, whether to sell stuff to the space people or to possible tourists, we don't know. Otherwise, the town remained pretty normal. In other words, the old panic argument is not a good one."

Bob added a little more mixer to the half-consumed drink and asked me if I had heard of the scare which citizens of a large midwestern town (not a city) experienced as a result of rumors about an atomic pile running out of control. I hadn't.

Stories were taken out of the paper after an early edition. Actually the pile hadn't run away at all. But there were rumors that radiation had raised in the vicinity and as a precaution CD leaders urged citizens to go to their basements. There was widespread panic, looting, all that bit. I could show you this private study our group made, but I don't have it along."

"But what of this Antarctica business? Who is responsible for these saucers anyhow?" I asked, impatiently. His story was beginning to make a little sense and he began to sound less and less like a crackpot.

"Bob" then pulled a small book from his briefcase. It was titled *"Agartha"* by a Buddhist lama named Robert Dickhoff. Then he looked at my library shelf and exclaimed, "Oh I see you don't have this. . .work."

I took it from his manner that he was being facetious.

"There is an occult tradition that the inside of the earth is inhabited. This finds expression in tales of Rainbow City, the Dero Hell, giants in the earth, and all of that. Of course occult tradition always contains some truth, but greatly distorted from reality.

"Do you remember the Admiral Byrd story?" he continued.

"Oh yes, something. About his flying over an uncharted territory and finding warm climate. Is there really something to this (Later Ray Palmer would publish the Admiral Byrd legend in his magazine, *Flying Saucers*, and it would arouse much controversy)?"

"A bit, yes, but this was greatly distorted. First of all, to my knowledge it didn't appear in any of the news media, but facts have a way of leaking out as scuttlebut. The fact is that on a certain flight Byrd did find all his charts confused. The temperature suddenly rose and he found himself flying in darkness. It was probably miraculous that he got out of this alive."

"You mean he flew into the center of the earth?"

"Of course not. What actually occurred is not fully understood. We don't really know too much about magnetism and the why of magnetic fields. It seems that the same phenomena which make our compasses work create a nagnetic field distortion somewhere near the geographic south pole. It seems that somebody entering this field would first find hinself in total darkness. Then, if he knew how to navigate the field, he would find himself in recognizable form of reality that would not be like our own. It is at the other side of this distortion field that the saucers originate."

My credulity momentarily decreased. This man was getting on the "4-D" kick, and that in my book was madness.

"You mean this *mat* and *demat* business?"

"You've been reading too much nut literature," the man replied.

"But suffice it to say there is a barrier there, which can be controlled or passed through with the correct technical know-how. Just what is on the other side nobody can be quite sure of. But the saucers originate there.

"Behind this field is a race of people civilized beyond all of our dreams. It is a very old race, about which there are many theories, which are not important to go into here, for if you published it, you would really sound way out."

The man suddenly rose. I looked at my watch. Although I have greatly condensed the conversation in the foregoing pages, I noted that he had talked exactly one hour.

"Hey," I remonstrated, "Why some silly rule about an hour when you're just started!"

He smiled. "I've given you all the keys. Let's see what you come up with."

"But you left out the *real* key. Sure, you say the saucers are from Antarctica, maybe a few from Mars and what not, but you haven't told me why they don't contact Earth people, what they are doing here. . ."

"You're trying to say that I didn't tell you the *WHY* of saucers. You see, the origin of saucers bothers nobody. People only set up concessions stands to sell the space people rebel flags. You have a great point there, Jim, and I want to see if you can come up with the rest of it. Call this a

psychological experiment. Call it a hoax, call me a Commie, anything. But I think you're convinced that it is the *WHY* of saucers that is important."

He finished off the drink, visited the bathroom and walked out with the renewed promise he'd contact me within two weeks.

As soon as he was out of the room, I ran to the window for I was suddenly consumed with a curiosity about the man who had visited me.

A large black Cadillac had pulled up near the entrance to the apartment building and a man, presumably a chauffeur, waited inside. Soon my friend Bob, appeared, the chauffeur got out, opened the door for him, and took a large brown suitcase from him and placed it in the trunk. They soon drove off. I'm sure this has no significance, but the man had no suitcase with him when he visited me. It probably contained some data he had thought about bringing in and had probably left outside the door. I'm sure the man didn't live in our apartment building for I have checked this out.

"Bob" left me in a really puzzled position. The import of it all, in fact, wouldn't hit me until a few days later, after I had published the following announcement in the October, 1954, issue of *Nexus*.

The information I have discussed so far is a matter of public record. However, just before this issue of *Nexus* went to press, I received irrefutable documented evidence which fully confirms these ideas.

". . .It is now too late to assemble this startling data for this present issue, but it will be presented in full in the November issue."

From my conversation with the visitor I had concluded, somewhat incorrectly, that if I wrote up the interview accurately, on his next visit he would reveal the rest of the mystery when he brought the photographs for me. Over the next two days, therefore, I did not concentrate on figuring out what the why of saucers might be, but on preparing an accurate report. I came up with fifteen pages, which I condensed to three, to fit into the limited format.

I had not expected another visit until two weeks later, the promised date for the delivery of the photographs. But just one week, to the day, the following Monday, my telephone rang at 11:00 A.M.

"Hi, buddy. Three guesses."

The midwestern voice was unmistakable.

"Bob!"

"Right!"

"Did you bring the cup to go with the saucer?" I asked, as a disguised question about the expected photographs.

"Well. . .*not exactly*. Say, Jim. I called to see if you were there. I have to see you, buddy."

I told him to give me fifteen minutes to get dressed, for I had overslept. He said he was in Manhattan and that it would be a little longer than that.

When Bob arrived he appeared tense and morose. Since he carried nothing with him, I knew he had not brought the photos. I had entertained the suspicion that I would never see them again.

"Jim," he began. "I'm about to welch on the deal. I don't want you to print the article."

I had started to hand it to him to inspect. He did not proffer his hand to take it.

"My conduct was inexcusable; you are under no obligation to kill your article. I can say that the article would get me into trouble. It probably would make you a laughing stock anyhow, if you did run it."

I did a real double take.

"Gee, thanks!" I exclaimed. I've already printed the issue in which I say I'll reveal the whole bit next issue. What will my readers think of me?"

"Jim, you do have a real problem. If I stuck my neck out again to help you solve it, I'd probably make the situation a whole lot worse."

"But why did you change your mind about the photos?"

"Believe me, Jim. The thing wouldn't be any good for you either."

I was getting hot under the collar, though I knew I would not use the material from my own volition, since he insisted on it. I still remembered the rules of ethics in journalism.

"You gave me this crackpot theory and got me half way to believing it. I published this notice in *Nexus*, and if I don't come up with something the readers will think I made up the whole thing trying to imitate Al Bender for publicity purposes."

"So you'll get publicity. But I'm sorry you'll have to get it this way."

"Let me get this straight now. You're not saying I *can't* print this but that it's simply off the record. Right?"

"Right," Bob said.

"O.K. It's killed. But I'll print anything I already knew before your first visit, and I'll have to find some way to get out from under the announcement I made. This is only a saucer magazine but somehow to me, it does represent the Fourth Estate and I'm serious about it.

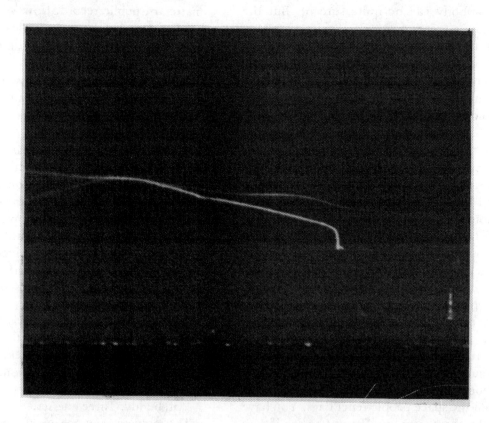

4:00
"The Solution To The Flying Saucer Mystery"

Regardless of what I personally thought about Gray Barker's book, *They Knew Too Much About Flying Saucers*, and the hard time Yonah and I were giving the author on the Long John Show that night, it had been one of the two books which had affected greatly my direction in UFO research during the next few years after their publication.

The other book was *The Report On Unidentified Flying Objects*, by the late Edward J. Ruppelt, who had been head of Project Blue Book at Wright-Patterson. (Doubleday and Co., Inc., Garden City, N.Y., 1956. Now out of print but copies available from Saucerian Books at $5.95.)

As soon as I had read the Ruppelt book I had suspicion that it had been set up. A personal interview with Ruppelt and a hastily improvised sequel to his book brought out four years later would tend to strengthen those suspicions.

I looked across microphones to observe Barker as he defended his book and his position on the *Saucer News* article. He looked and sounded too sincere to be a conscious tool of any government pressure. I also had gotten to know him personally, and many conversations with him had also convinced me that, though a bit too credulous with the wild claims he published, here was a man tremendously enthusiastic about solving the flying saucer mystery, as it had grown to be called—though a man who sometimes let his enthusiasm get away with him.

His theory that flying saucer researchers had been silenced, combined with my own deliberate suppression of the promised article, convinced many people that I, also, had been hushed by the three men in black.

Long John's impish business about the spelling of my name on my apartment directory, Barker's digging out the letter "proving" my tenure in the air force, and the veiled suggestions that I was in the pay of the Silence Group (a term coined by Maj. Donald E. Keyhoe in his books), were all echoes of public reaction after Barker's book hit the stores.

The book had been tremendously popular, both in sales and reader acceptance. Some people claimed they had become terrified and couldn't sleep after reading it, but nevertheless went about buying copies for friends. People wrote me after reading it, accusing me of being a member of the air force, the Silence Group, and the CIA.

If I could at all believe in the part of the book outlining the visit to Bender by the Three Men, it was in the framework of a possible hoax. Lonzo Dove's *Saucer News* which we were discussing suggested this idea, though it went much too far. If a hoax, Barker had been drawn into it also and was an innocent victim.

When Bob had visited me with his fascinating photographs, and for a year or two afterward, I entertained seriously the idea that he had been a government agent, whether with the military or some civilian intelligence group. That was one of the reasons I had clammed up about the matter and had not even discussed it with colleagues in UFO research. Regardless of how much I wanted to print everything I knew, I was still patriotic, whether or not government policies were realistic or right.

Then came the realization, especially after the publication of Barker's Book, that I had been the victim of a hoax, as Bender might have been. I had often discussed possible hoaxes with Barker. Although he agreed there was some possibility, and that Bender could no doubt have been fooled, still he couldn't find the *motivation* for such actions, regardless of how he racked his brain.

The part of Ruppelt's book which had impressed me most was the chapter titled "The Radiation Story," pages 263-264. This was strangely similar to the ideas which Bob had expressed in our strange interview.

Bob had given me a really wild story, though with fairly good detail, about an Antarctic origin for saucers. The gist of his conversation also gave me the impression that he believed that the public would *not* panic if they heard that flying saucers were real, but that there *was* a great potential danger of panic which might result from a rumor or announcement about serious radiation threats (i.e. his example, whether fabricated or real, about the two towns and their reactions to rumors of both saucers and radiation).

Ruppelt's narrative strangely tied in. In the chapter mentioned above Ruppelt repeated 'Bob's' story, almost word for word, as to how several teams of highly qualified scientists proved that the background radiation content of the atmosphere increased sharply on several occasions at the same time a flying saucer was observed visually in the vicinity of the radiation measuring equipment.

Although I had promised Bob I would not reveal his information, I was severely tempted to break my word in the light of Ruppelt's printing some of the same information.

Even then, more than a year later, readers and friends were still pressuring me to tell what I had found out.

I had really found out *nothing* which was definite, though Bob had given me some ideas which nagged at the back of my mind. I might have come up with some clue to the saucer mystery, though a very small part of it.

I don't know if I made the right decision, but anyhow I decided to do something about it. If I created and published an article *purporting* to tell what I knew it probably would accomplish two purposes. It would get the public off my back and would serve as a trial balloon to determine whether I had something or not. If Bob had been a government representative, such an article likely would bring some reaction and I might have at least some indication of the validity of these theories.

Even today, I still believe that one vital clue to the origin and propulsion of saucers is the radiation that is associated with them, though certainly not necessarily within the framework of the article I published.

In preparing the article I took a far-out premise.

Many researchers and saucer enthusiasts who had been concerned about the radiation accompanying saucers, had been confusing cause and effect. Maybe saucers didn't *cause* radiation, but radiation, in some round about way, *caused saucers*!

What if saucers really did originate at the South Pole, either based there from an interplanetary or intergalactic source to escape detection, or built by some fantastic dero-ish or Rainbow City race there? What if their main concern was the dangerous radiation caused by our bomb tests? They might be measuring the ever-increasing radiation or trying to nullify it.

True, the theory was fantastic and possibly crackpot, but it also sounded as sensible as many of the others which had been advanced.

Dr. D. had told me that the scientific community, at the request of the government, was deliberately playing down the radiation dangers. The serious problem of the increasing radiation was confirmed by President John F. Kennedy, after he had successfully negotiated a nuclear test ban with the Soviet Union and other nations.

But what if Bob were correct, and that public knowledge of the seriousness of the radiation danger would cause panic? I should tread on this subject with caution. I therefore decided that it would be expedient to partially deceive my readers. Whether I did right or wrong will not be known until more progress is made toward a final solution of the saucer mystery.

Let me say that I still believe that the article, titled "The Solution to the Flying Saucer Mystery," which appeared in the June-July, 1956, issue of *Saucer News*, did contain a great deal of fact, though disguised.

In commenting on the chapter in Ruppelt's book, I told my readers, "I can tell you that this radiation clue *is* correct, and very important.

Ruppelt does not know it, but the type of saucers that the Government particularly does not want us to know about, run on atomic energy, and they operate by means of this combination—which, of course, represents an entirely new and previously unknown type of propulsion. They vary in size from about 6 to 30 feet in diameter, and they are remotely controlled, as a human being probably could not survive in these highly radioactive machines.

Research on this type of saucer was being done as early as 1946, and its startlingly advanced design and performance represents an improvement over earlier experimental saucer-shaped aircraft. These saucers are capable of speeds in excess of 4,000 miles per hour, and are also capable of hovering, changing course abruptly, and all the other performance characteristics that are usually attributed to saucers.

Then, switching what I had been told of Antarctica to a U.S. location, I stated, "This type of saucer operates from a *supersecret underground base* in one of our Southwestern states, and is being sent out over the country from there—and overseas, as well.

The whole project is so highly classified that ordinary military pilots and even the air force's saucer investigators on Project Blue Book could not possibly know about it. In .fact, this type of saucer is not built by the American government as we ordinarily understand the word government. As fantastic as this may sound to you, these saucers are actually built, operated, and maintained by an organization which is entirely separate from the military and political branches of the Government that we know about. Although a handful of people at the very top of the Government know about the existence of this project, they have no direct connection with it. In the remainder of this article, I shall call this secret project "The Organization."

The main reason for the fantastic secrecy surrounding this project is not because of the new type of propulsion involved. The key to the saucer riddle is not *what* are the saucers, but *the purpose* for their operation. People naturally wonder why, if the saucers are American devices—why are they sent up over cities and other areas where people can see them, and where they would supposedly endanger civilian lives if they crashed or went out of control. The reason is that 'The Organization' has no choice in the matter. These saucers were originally designed to test, in machines capable of very high speeds, the heat resistence of the metals that would later be used in the construction of larger rocket-shaped craft that would travel at lower speeds within our atmosphere, and which would use another, less dangerous system of power. But these cigar-shaped craft are another story, outside the scope of this article. The important fact is that the saucers, originally built primarily for the purpose stated above, were found to be far more vital for another purpose—*that of absorbing excess radioactivity in our atmosphere.*

This is the service they are now performing, and this is why the people of the United States have not been told about the very existence of the saucers—for "The Organization" could not tell us without revealing the fearful purpose that these machines are serving. The truth is that one or more of our secret tests involving atomic energy got decidedly out of hand. The atmosphere has been polluted to a dangerous and alarming degree. (In considering the above statement, please remember that not all atomic tests involve bombs; there are others which do not have anything to do with bombs.)

The saucers run on a small atomic plant. As they pass through or hover in a given area, they absorb radiation from the atmosphere. This they convert into what I will call, for lack of a better technical term, electrical energy. (I do not feel it necessary or advisable to go into technical details on this.) Thus, when a dangerously radioactive cloud is over a certain area, one or more saucers are sent to that area for the specific purpose of absorbing this excess. If the cloud happens to be over a populated area, there is all the more reason to proceed with the job of decontaminating it. If the cloud is over a foreign country, there is as much reason to absorb its excess radioactivity as if it were over the United States.

The saucers cannot absorb all the radioactivity in a given area, but they can reduce it to below the dangerous level. After a given flight, they return to their base for servicing; but at times it occurs that a saucer becomes "saturated" with radioactivity and is too dangerous even to return to the base. If this happens, then it is sent out over the ocean and directed down into the sea, at one of the deepest parts of the ocean. Thus the rate of replacement of these craft is fairly high. However, their cost of operation is extremely low, and their range and power supply are practically limitless. By their construction, no saucer of this type can land or come closer than a few feet to the ground; nor can one crash on the ground even if it should go out of control. An automatic destruction mechanism causes it to disintegrate in flight. if necessary. Similarly, a device which for want of a better term I shall call "reverse radar" prevents them from crashing into objects to which they fly near, such as airplanes. During flight, these saucers operate partly by remote guidance, and partly by an extremely complex system of automatic devices within the machine itself.

These saucers make very little noise in flight, because they ionize the air in front of them, and minimize air friction as they fly along. Because of their electrical nature, they glow in the dark, and

REPLY TO
ATTN OF:

SUBJECT:

Response for Request of Information in Relation to UFO Contact and
Other Related information

TO:

Len Stringfield

1. In January of 1978, I was station at McGuire AFB, N.J.. One evening , during the
time frame of 0300hrs. and 0500hrs., there were a number of UFO sightins in the area over
the air field and Ft. DIX Army camp. I am a security policeman and was on routine patrol
at the time. N.J. State Police, and Ft. Dix MP's were runnig code in the direction of
Brownsville,N.J.. A state trooper then entered Gate #5 at the rear of the base requestin
assistance and permission to enter. I was dispatched and the trooper wanted access to the
runway area which led to the very back of the air field and connected with a heavily wooded area which is part of the Dix training area. He informed me that a Ft. Dix MP was
pursueing a low flying object which then hovered over his car. He described it as oval
shaped, with no details, and glowing with a blueish green color. His radio transmission
was cut off. At that time in front of his police car, appeared a thing, about 4ft. tall,
greyish, brown, fat head, long arms, and slender body. The MP panicked and fired five
rounds from his .45 Cal into the thing, and one round into the object above. The object
then fled straight up and joined with eleven others high in the sky. This we all saw
but didn't know the details at the time. Anyway, The ting ran into the woods towards our
fenceline and they wanted to look for it. By this time several patrols were involved.

2. We found the body of the thing near the runway. It had apparently climbed the fence
and died while running. It was all of a sudden hush-hush and no one was allowed near
the area. We roped off the area and AF CSI came out and took over. That was the last I
saw of it. There was a bad stench coming from it too. Like ammonia smelling but it
wasn't constent in the air. That day, a team from Wright-Patterson AFB came in a C141
and went to the area. They crated it in a wooden box, sprayed something over it, and then
put it into a bigger metal container. They loaded it in the plane and took off. That
was it, nothing more said, no report made and we were all told not to have anything to
say about it or we would be court martialed.

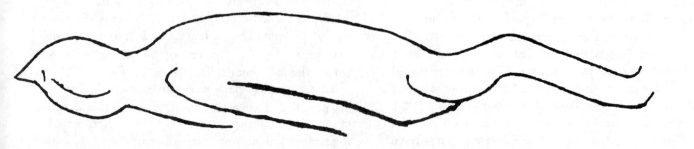

when photographed in daylight they do not show a sharply defined outline. Because of the fact that they overload the atmosphere with electricity, they are the cause of many thunderstorms, and of much of the unusually perverse weather we have had during the past few years. They are usually flown over populated areas at night if possible, and "The Organization" is happiest when they are not seen often or from close range. However, the purpose they serve is so important that it is merely a "calculated risk" if the saucers occasionally cause an air accident or a mild panic—as in the summer of 1952, when the necessity of having saucers fly over Washington D.C. caused an unusually high amount of speculation as to their nature. But anything is preferable to allowing this radiation to go unchecked.

"The Organization" knows the panic that would follow if the public were to realize the fact that the atmosphere is dangerously contaminated. Perhaps damage too great to undo has already been done, or possibly this radiation is still out of control, and will continue to get worse until or unless some new and better method is invented to cope with it. I believe that the saddest thing of all is that all this has been going on—the pollution of the atmosphere and the attempted control of this pollution by the saucers—without the public knowing anything about it. This shows just how far the people have lost touch with the technical advances of our Nation. While the battle for our survival against radiation poisoning is going on secretly in the skies above us, we continue to maintain our Economy b y b u i l d i n g a l m o s t a s m a n y conventionally propelled aircraft as ever—the ones we all read about and see overhead every day. And the public is never the wiser!

Even the nation's top rocket experts seem to have been kept in the dark about saucers in the early days—*until* it became necessary for them to know about them. I said earlier in this article that the saucers were originally designed to make tests that would eventually lead to the construction of large rocket-shaped craft. Some of these larger have already been constructed. Willy Ley, one of the world's outstanding authorities on rockets, stated publicly on April 7, 1950, that his personal opinion is that the saucers are a United States military secret. But on April 22, 1956, the same

Willy Ley stated that he is convinced that "nothing is being surpressed by the Air Force except the names and addresses of the multitudes reporting saucers." In other words, he no longer *claims* to believe that saucers are U.S. made. Why is it that, of recent years, every top scientist or engineer who has made a public statement of saucers either claims to believe they do not exist, or that they are extraterrestial? Why do they not suggest or even consider the "Earth Theory" in public anymore? Are these men being sincere, or are they covering up something of vital importance to all of us?

In closing, I wish to point out that I do not claim to have discussed *all* flying saucers in this article. There are other unconventional craft being built by this country for other purposes. Some of these are saucer-shaped and some cigar-shaped—and quite a few are piloted. There are also *unidentified* flying objects, which have been seen for many, many years, and perhaps even for centuries. These latter may or may not include space ships from other planets. What I have discussed in this article is the type of saucer which is the cause of all the secrecy. It is this type, and its purpose, that 'The Organization' does not want you to know about. In short, this type is the 'key' to the saucer mystery.

Reaction by my readers to the above article were unexpected and definite. They not only disliked and disbelieved the article, but more and more expressed their belief that I was a secret AF of CIA agent, trying to lead them away from the truth.

Not wishing to back down from my article, and still not wishing to reveal just why I had written it, I continued to employ subterfuge as the editorial policy of *Saucer News* continued to emphasize what came to be widely referred to in the UFO press as Moseley's Earth Theory.

There probably is still a minor part of my Earth Theory which I developed over the years in *Saucer News* which may be of some value to UFO research. I am also convinced that the ideas to be found in the many articles on this subject represent only a small part of the total UFO mystery.

My confidence in the Earth Theory and my cynicism about hush-ups began to crumble one night on the Long John show. It started with a telephone call and ended in near panic.

4:30
Hush-up!

Some day I may actually ask Long John just what happened on his show that morning.

Probably it wouldn't be fair. I doubt if he would give me the answers anyhow. He probably knows, more than I and the other panel members know, what actually happened. But I doubt if he knows everything involved.

It almost seems that somewhere there is a shadowy Establishment, or Entrenchment, which would like to keep the saucer mystery, just as it is today, unsolved. But in its zeal this Establishment does not always handle things wisely. It is probably bogged down with red tape, with its own weight and incompetent representatives who do not understand psychology.

I think it slipped up on that particular morning.

Long John had been obviously enjoying the leg-pulling I had been taking as a result of the mispelling of my name and the boondoggled air force letter. One of the panel members, however, seemed to be taking this with a seriousness inappropriate to the mood of the discussion.

As a result the show once more got around to my possible involvement as a former member of the air force or as a secret government agent.

As we talked Long John had moved back from his microphone, turned his face aside, and was whispering into the telephone, as he often did when he conferred with the producer and others in the control room. Since this was such a routine action I did not notice any particular facial reaction or mood he may have expressed during his conversation. I only know that he was on the intercom phone before he interrupted our conversation:

"I think, gentlemen," John abruptly told us, "it would be advisable at this point if we forget the air force letter. We'll just drop this completely."

One of the panel members objected to the decision and persisted in the same line of questioning.

"Would you do me a favor, Ben?"

John's voice had taken a strange tone. He was either frightened, or angry. His fingers tensed where he held the next commercial. He was disguising his feelings but I could tell one thing: Long John was shaken.

The shocked panel member had turned to John. *"Let's drop the subject!"*

There was such firmness in John's voice that the studio immediately became deathly quiet, except for the subliminal sound of the subject dropping like a ton of bricks.

Yonah was the first to collect his wits and change the subject. He asked Barker a question.

I was still stunned. I wondered what was going on. If I was certain of nothing else I knew that if the audio had conveyed the happening realistically to the listener that I would no longer be able to convince *anybody* that I was not an agent of some kind.

If somebody or some organization was stopping the questioning of myself, it certainly was without my own knowledge or participation. In fact, I had been rather enjoying playing the man of mystery.

I had even confused Capt. Edward J. Ruppelt himself, still without intention or saucers aforethought.

Shortly after his book had come out I visited him in California where he lived. I had learned of his whereabouts from a television producer and rang him up. He seemed affable and quite willing to talk with me.

But my first impression of Ruppelt, aside from his intelligence and pleasant personality was the suspicion that he seemed to entertain of me and which he couldn't completely hide. I got the distinct impression that Ruppelt, himself, former head of Project Bluebook, and titular leader of the official Air Force party line, thought I was an agent who had come to check up on him!

After a while Ruppelt must have at least partially abandoned this mistrust, for he opened up somewhat and I must say that I was amazed at what he told me.

Not that he gave me any secret information. I am now convinced that practically everything Ruppelt really knew about saucers was contained in his book. Since there was a great deal in the conversation which was either personal or off the record, let me get over this particular subject by saying that my main impression of Ruppelt was that he was an ardent saucer believer! Whether his book, one of the most sensible and definitive in its area ever published, was heavily edited, or whether he had the good sense to tone down his own beliefs, I don't know.

The most amazing thing about his enthusiasm was his great interest in contactees. After his initial mistrust of me abated, I spent most of our interview not asking him questions, but giving him data I had collected on the contactees and especially on the little men.

I was well equipped to brief Ruppelt on the "little men," for though they bordered on the "contactee" area which I disbelieved and mistrusted, the subject to me had always been a fascinating one. To me it seemed pretty logical that if, indeed, saucers were interplanetary, the creatures or people piloting them might be very unlike Earth people. In fact they likely would appear quite grotesque.

One of my most interesting cases on file involved a twelve-year-old boy who lived in Coldwater, Kansas, who maintained he saw a strange looking little man climb out of a flying saucer in a corn field.

"I was on our farm, sitting on the tractor," John Jacob Sqaim told an investigator for *Nexus*, "when suddenly I saw him, about twenty feet away. He stood right there, a little fellow about the size of a 5-year-old child. He had long, pointed ears, and a pointed nose. He was sort of crouching, looking at me. Then he ran—or maybe flew—to the saucer."

Until then the boy hadn't seen the saucer, which was hidden behind a terrace. It was hanging about five feet from the ground. Then the little man jumped into a door and the saucer took off.

"It went awfully fast—so fast that compared to it, a jet would seem like a turtle."

The boy's father said that he questioned the boy closely and then called the sheriff, who advised the family to stay away from the scene, and found weird, pear-shaped footprints there. It was the sheriff's opinion that the boy might have been deluded as to seeing the saucer—but he could not explain the mysterious footprints.

Meanwhile, one saucer that didn't land, but made a dramatic enough story just being in the air, was reported in Lisbon, Portugal by a landowner named Cesar Feriera. This man had seen not a flying saucer, but a flying *cup*, complete with "two eight-foot giants clad in pocketless metallic suits."

A "little man" saucer landing scare pervaded France. In Quarouble a steelworker claimed that a small flying saucer paid him a visit and that two armless men in space helmets came out for a look around. When he ran out of his house for a closer look, a bright light seemed to paralyze him, and the strange machine made a clean getaway.

The steelworker, Maurice DeWilde, had been reading a book in his kitchen when his dog became aware of the visitors and began to bark. The Frenchman then peered out the window and saw a "black mass" on a nearby railway line. When he hurriedly flicked on his flashlight, he saw two little little creatures about three feet tall.

The little men had wide shoulders, normal legs, but no arms; and each had something that looked like a space helmet on his head. When DeWilde ran toward them, a bright green light from the machine temporarily blinded him.

He described the saucer to police as shaped like a cake cover, about eighteen feet in diameter.

Suddenly the object rose, with a cloud of black smoke hissing from it. Police found marks where the saucer had landed.

As I took out a large envelope containing the first mailing from a foreign press clipping service to which I had recently subscribed, I could see that Ruppelt was impressed, I did not mention to him the large fee I had paid for the service, which indicated that the landing "flap" had certainly hit its peak in Europe, unequalled since the concentration during 1952 in this country!

From Belgium, Spain, Portugal, England, France, Norway and Austria the clipping service had dug up strange reports.

In Muenster, Germany, a movie projectionist, Franz Hoge, told the news agency DPA that he saw a saucer land and peculiarly-shaped creatures get out of it. They were only three and a half feet tall, and wore rubber-like clothing.

One of the rare photos of flying saucer occupants was taken by Giampiere Monguzzi, on July 31, 1952, while on vacation in the Bermina Mountains, Italy. Photograph above shows a being who had just emerged from the saucer when surprised by the witness. Below are greatly enlarged portions of the above and another photo, showing the little man in greater detail. Feet have been sketched in to give some idea of height.

From Castelibranco, Portugal came the story of four men who saw two tall aluminum-clad figures emerge from a grounded saucer. The saucermen picked flowers, collected twigs and shrubs, as if gathering scientific information.

Not only were the odd beings scientific, but hospitable as well, for they invited, by means of gestures, the observers to come aboard their ship to look inside it. When their invitation was, somewhat understandably, declined, the creatures boarded their craft and took off vertically at unbelievable speed.

A mail carrier in the Belgium village of Hmy, spotted a saucer near the ground, and claimed to have seen two silhouettes, "roughly human in shape," aboard the machine.

From Chatterlerault, France, came the story of Yves David, who said his arm was carressed by a little creature dressed in a space suit and who talked unintelligibly, paralyzed him with a green ray, and then ran off to his saucer.

In Bugeat, France, Antoine Mazaud had a similar experience, with a man described as "normal looking," who came up to him, kissed him, mumbled unintelligible words, and then retreated to his saucer (about 10 feet long and cigar shaped).

Also from France was a report by a Madame Leboeuf, of Drome, who said that a man in a "plastic outfit" come toward her and frightened her. As she ran in fright he took off vertically in his craft. The machine sounded like a musical top as it left, she reported.

One of the clippings, from Perpigan, France, told how a retired French custom official saw a saucer land and a tall man, dressed in a diver's suit, step out. The Frenchman, Damien Sigueres, described the saucer as a large red sphere. Suddenly the saucerian saw Sigueres' two dogs and hastily retreated into the machine. Another attitude was expressed by two other saucerians, who petted a Monsieur Garrau's dog. These two men were dressed in Khaki.

So far the creatures had either said nothing or used strange language, but in Perpigan, France, it seemed that the strange visitors had mastered at least a smattering of the language—and even employed terrestrial fuels in their machines. A railroad worker discovered a saucer pilot next to a Deisel oil tank, and asked the space man, who was either covered with hair or was wearing a long, hairy overcoat, what he wanted. Although the man's language was incomprehensible to the Frenchman, he distinctly picked out the word, "gasoil."

The story had it that the workman ran off to report the incident to the stationmaster—we don't know whether it was to get permission to sell the man some "gasoil" but suspect that it was due to fright—but before he had gone 100 yards, the strange machine took off and vanished.

In general, Frenchmen were taking the reports very seriously and near panic was said to have pervaded some provinces. It may have been just Gallic humor, but the mayor of the village of ChateauNeuf-du-Pape issued a decree forbidding flying saucers to land, and ordered the local constable to impound any which disobeyed. The decree stated that such strange aircraft "would be of a nature to disturb public order and the tranquility of the inhabitants," most certainly an understatement!

An innkeeper in Brittany placed an advertisement in his local paper, offering $35,000 to anyone who would bring him a Martian alive. I had no follow-up to this story, but presumed it was as unsuccessful as my own publicly announced $1,000 reward to anybody who could provide me with "concrete, material proof that flying saucers are visiting Earth from other planets."

Another saucerman managed to mumble something that at least sounded intelligent, to wit, "I'll be seeing you," to Jean Narcy, a road mender of Haute-Marne, France. The man was riding to work on his bicycle when he spotted a little whiskered man in a wheat field just under four feet tall. After saying this goodbye the man got in his saucer and took off with a buzzing sound.

A Breton baker, a Monsieur Pierre-Lucas, said that a Martian had asked him for a light, but didn't remember what language he used.

But one of the weirdest Martians was the one who stopped Roger Barrault near the town of Lavous. The creature had brilliant eyes, an enormous mustache, wore rubbers and spoke Latin.

But that was not as marvelous as the sight a traveling salesman witnessed in the Cotes-du-Nord district: a deep rose colored flying saucer from which stepped a zebra-striped man. As he alighted, he changed color, chameleon-like, from yellow to green!

Another packet of clippings contained numerous French landing reports: In Vron two youths stumbled across a flying saucer as they returned from work. "Strange little men" were clustered around it, but as soon as the youths drew near, the little men hurried back inside and the saucer took off. A "moon-shaped" machine, a new configuration in the French landings, touched down near Lusignac; at Poncey-sur-Lignon, a small village near Dijon, a saucer landed and left strange markings on the ground. The markings were examined by the entire village, and photographed. Another landing, at Diges, was witnessed by Gisele Finns, a fifteen-year-old farm girl, who said "the pilot looked just like men who live around here." Some children at Sainte Claude watched the landing of a saucer "of such a vivid color that it looked like the metal was burning up." They described the occupant as looking "like a giant lump of sugar." Two inhabitants of Lezignan saw a disc thirty feet in diameter land in a field between the villages of Lagrasse and Aude. When they approached it, the machine flashed a blinding light on them, and made the usual getaway. In Megrit, a farmer named Henri Lehrisse saw a small machine only one yard in diameter in his courtyard. Inside were two human forms, which looked like children.

I had rather definitely come to a negative conclusion on the so-called "contactees," I told Ruppelt. As Long John would put it, I certainly didn't "buy" them.

Some of the little men sightings, I pointed out,

were just as suspect. For example, one report had two Frenchmen seeing two strange little creatures standing next to a saucer-shaped machine. At first something about the clipping seemed to strike me, but it wasn't until I had read it several times that I discovered that, translated into English, the name of the man telling of the adventure was "Blind"; the name of the man who allegedly saw the saucer translated was "Liar"; and the place where the incident was "House of Liars."

Another Frenchman, a restaurant proprietor, reported that while motorcycling between the towns of Toulon and Heyeres, he saw a man who stepped out of a saucer, and asked him, "Are you a Martian?"—to which the man, dressed in overalls, replied, "No, I am French. Where am I?"

Although many of the "little men" reports were obviously full of hot air, the multitude of them contained some logic.

Many of the little men seemed merely to be carrying out scientific investigations, such as gathering samples of soil, vegetation and so on. They seemed generally to avoid contact with "natives," as our own astronauts might, should they land on Mars and find intelligent creatures there—at least until they found that the Martians harbored no dangerous germs.

I told Ruppelt of my investigation of one similar incident, though it didn't involve a little man, but a monsterous looking "Head man"; and despite the fact that I had to suggest it was a hoax to get permission to publish the picture I think it is a pretty good case, considering the caliber of the witnesses involved.

I still can't give the names of the witnesses; suffice it to say that they were members of a certain South American embassy returning to their own country for a vacation at home.

Five of these people told me that shortly out of Miami a gleaming disc shaped object approached their plane and flew alongside, at very close range. The pilot, in a shaky voice, got on the intercom and advised the passengers there was an unidentified flying object flying close to the port side, but to "not be alarmed," because that in the past such objects had not shown hostility.

"I don't want to try to get away from it for it's too close to our wing and I'm afraid to maneuver. I'm sure it will soon go away after looking at us for a while.

"Meanwhile our stewardesses will give you a cup of coffee to go with the flying saucer, if you like," he continued, apparently hoping that a bit of humor would ease the fear and curiosity of the passengers.

The five people were seated in the same area, directly opposite the saucer. People were straining to see the thing, and the stewardess firmly told them to remain seated and to fasten their seat belts.

"It was a cigar-shaped object, half as long as our plane," one of the men stated. "It had no visible antenna, landing gear or anything like that, and no windows, until a large port suddenly appeared as if it were fading in like a movie scene.

"Then peering at us from the port we saw a horrifying thing, Senor Moseley. It is impossible to describe, except as you might say it was a large head or brain with terrible tentacles."

I managed to talk with all five people, in separate interviews, and all of their accounts substantially agreed. One of the witnesses did the mentioned sketch.

These people apparently had no reason to perpetrate a hoax, and had good reason to request that I withhold their names.

The postscript to this story is also strange. After the cigar-shaped craft pulled away and vanished at great speed, the pilot mentioned he would make a non-scheduled stop in Ecuador, "to pick up a diplomat of high standing."

As soon as the plane had taxied to a stop, several men in American Air Force uniforms hurried to the cockpit and met the South American pilot, engaging him in animated conversation. He accompanied them into an area other than the passenger entrance to the airport.

Several ambulances had been driven up to the landing area. As soon as the passengers embarked, a man, dressed in what apparently was a protective suit to protect him from radiation, climbed into the cockpit and taxied the plane away. The passengers were taken to the VIP lounge, an official entered and read from a paper. His spiel went something like this, as well as the witnesses could remember:

"Welcome to the————Airlines office in Ecuador. We are pleased to have you stopping here. You will soon be departing on another aircraft, since we are not equipped to refuel the aircraft you arrived in.

"During your flight I am advised you had the unique experience of seeing an experimental Russian aircraft. They are very sorry about its unauthorized approach to the plane and have cabled their apologies. The pilot will be severely reprimanded."

Ruppelt told me he had never heard of the

report, but appeared to be greatly interested in it. He pointed out, and logically, that a helmeted pilot, with goggles and oxygen apparatus which may not have been seen too clearly through the port, could have been misinterpreted by nervous passengers. They certainly had a right to be nervous, I agreed, during such a close approach of another aircraft, whether terrestrial or UFO. The porthole could have appeared suddenly, having been unseen due to reflections.

But the obvious concern over radiation made the story very interesting, he admitted, regardless of who or what the "headman" was.

Ruppelt insisted that I visit him the next time I was on the West Coast, where he had taken up residence. Unfortunately I did not have an opportunity to do so, for a year or so later the former Captain, though a very young man, died of a heart attack.

Many questions, which Ruppelt could no doubt answer, remain mysteries. The chief question is why his book was revised after I talked with him, and after it had already played out, as far as sales went. A huge edition was printed but few were sold. Had the original edition been too greatly "pro saucer" for the AF's stomach?

I have pieced together what actually happened that morning on the Long John Show from three sources: a tape recording of the broadcast; my own personal remembrances, reinforced by talking with Yonah; and Gray Barker's reporting of the matter in his column, "Chasing the Flying Saucers," in Ray Palmer's *Flying Saucers* magazine, December, 1959.

The tape recording at the point of the famous cut-off has the subject of hush-ups being argued hot and heavily. Long John is addressing Gray Barker:

JOHN: Did anyone ever hush *YOU* up?

BARKER: No, I. . . .

JOHN: Did you mention in one of your recent magazine articles about the possibility of hushing Long John, and was it written in one of the Palmer magazines that Long John will be hushed up or. . . .

Gray Barker's column, mentioned above, picks up the narrative at this point.

Suddenly music filled the studio as Long John jumped up angrily. For some unknown reason we had been cut off the air, and recorded music had been substituted. John ran into the control room where we could see, but not hear, his excited discussion with the engineer. The producer of the show then entered the studio and said slowly to another official, "It's serious this time."

Neither I nor the panel members were let in on what was going on. In answer to a question by Moseley, Long John replied only with, "You've seen what you have seen. I don't know any more myself."

We drew the producer aside and tried to question him.

" 'All I can say is,' he told us, 'that a voice which I knew, and knew to represent proper authority, was on the phone, and the voice ordered me to give the phone to the engineer. Let me say this—that the voice represented enough authority to be able to order the engineer to cut the program off and fill with music.'

"Then John instructed the producer how to answer all calls, especially those from regular panel members who would be calling up to find out what had gone wrong.

" 'When they call, tell them that John hasn't been feeling well all morning, that he had a slight headache, and planned to end the show an hour early and play music during the remaining time. Say that the engineer made a mistake and cut the show too early, and that I'm giving them all kinds of hell over it.'

"Then Long John cut into the music and made an announcement, stating that the program had been interrupted because of reasons beyond his control. We could sense that the staff wanted us out of there, so we left the studio and went our separate ways, after a hurried conference in the lobby, trying to figure out what had happened."

In his magazine story, Barker probably had good reason to limit his reporting of what occurred at the doorway of the lobby. In clearing the story with Long John he had been asked to report the matter truthfully but to avoid, if possible, reporting of the public reaction which followed.

A man who evidently was one of the elevator operators was assisting a night watchman in moving a heavy packing box against the main doorway. Outside a crowd of people had gathered: evidently listeners who had been up or driving in New York at that time. Probably imagining all sorts of things that might be happening to Long John, they had come to the studio to see what they could do and to engage in loud protest. Among the people were perhaps a half dozen reporters who held up notebooks on which they had scrawled *News, Tribune, Post* and so on. But the doors were being barricaded against everybody.

Dave Field, the producer, had followed us to the lobby and became our rescuer.

Years later, in 1964, the famous night of the power failure in New York, Barker and I again ran into Dave Field when, on a mutual dare, we would enter the same studio and walk up the labrythine stairways to the same 24th floor, using book matches for guidance.

On the night of the "hush-up" Dave led us through a ground-floor labrynth to a freight entrance and told us to get home as fast as we could manage.

I got my car at the parking lot two blocks away. Ordinarily I would have driven back around the front entrance of the studio to see just what was going on then, but frankly all three of us, Yonah, Barker and myself, were scared.

What dangerous line of discussion were we pursuing or leading into at the time of the cutoff? What had we said earlier on the show which had made the Silence Group jittery?

We dropped Yonah off in Brooklyn. Barker and I continued the discussion as I drove him to his uptown hotel. Barker grew silent and I knew he was thinking, trying to figure the situation.

"I'll get some sleep, and call you this afternoon. Maybe we can come up with something then," Barker told me as I let him out.

I turned the block and headed back down town, for I had suddenly decided to drive by the studio once again to see if the crowd had dispersed.

As I neared the location I met some police cars, their red lights still blinking; two of them were paddy wagons though I could not see inside them.

Silence reigned in front of the studio. One lone cop walked slowly by the doorway.

I circled the block and headed back through Times Square, on the way to the West Side Highway and home to Fort Lee, New Jersey.

The Crossroads-of-the-World had a haggard and eerie look. The neon had gone out and dawn was breaking. Pieces of newspaper, and other debris from the previous night flew about, whipped up by a rising wind.

I wondered if everything was as unreal as this, if there had actually been a Long John Show.

I switched on the radio. The music was still there, but it was fading.

"This is Long John again, we're going to wrap it up for another morning. I'm sorry that we ran into some difficulty, and I'll be back with you. . .again. . .tonight, I hope. . .'

A staggering drunk started to step off the sidewalk in front of my car, and I screeched to a stop. He fell, staggered to his feet, then walked in sidewise motion. The man, dishevelled, had an odd look, a strange look of youth just fading away. I looked again and saw long blonde hair, like that of a prophet, falling around his shoulders. The man, obviously one of the characters that frequent Times Square, was reminiscent of the Venusians we had discussed, and probably just as far out as were they.

I backed up, swerved and passed him. The near miss had shaken me. I was tired. I had slept little the night before the show, having stayed up late discussing saucers with Barker.

The George Washington Bridge loomed in the distance, shrouded in fog. The radio blanked out an awful buzzing came through, probably due to some local electrical interference. I turned it off. Maybe we were fooling around with a dangerous subject. Maybe Bender *hadn't* been hoaxed. Maybe my strange visitor, Bob had been *more* than a hoaxter or a government agent. Maybe I should drop UFO research.

Somehow, I mused, there was something to saucers that all of our theories and collecting of sighting accounts and investigations hadn't managed to cope with. There was very much still hidden. The saucer mystery seemed to be more vastly complex than one could ever imagine.

Then, suddenly, a penetrating understanding seemed to hit me and course through all my body. For a moment I had the *real* solution to the flying saucer mystery! Then the complex understanding faded as soon as it had filled my mind.

"But I still have a *fact*!" I almost shouted to myself.

Ray Palmer claimed to have such a *fact*. Like Ray, I felt that the possession of this *fact* would enable me to more thoroughly analyze reports and theories in the UFO field.

Then I knew that despite the many unknown quantities and potentially dangerous facets of deeply exploring the UFO mystery, *I would go on, hot and heavy, pursuing the elusive discs*. Whatever they were, I knew they could change the course of history.

In the meantime I would reveal my *fact* to nobody.

AT LAST!—THESE MAY BE LONG LOST "ALIEN PHOTOS" TAKEN AT THE SITE OF THE ROSWELL, NEW MEXICO, UFO CRASH CASE

A report © 1991 by Antonio Huneeus

During the last few months, at least two photographs purporting to show the remains of an extraterrestrial pilot found at the scene of the world-famous Roswell, New Mexico, UFO crash site has been circulated within international scientific and UFOlogical circles.

The alien photo was first revealed to the world during the second "Dialogue with the Universe" International UFO Conference, organized by Michael Hessemann in Munich in June of 1990. There, Marina Popovich, one of Russia's leading UFOlogists, released the photograph, claiming that she had received it from the late Professor Felix Zigel, who in turn had obtained it from a Canadian source.

The late Dr. Felix Yurevich Zigel, who passed away in December of 1988, was a lecturer in astronomy, physics and mathematics at the prestigious Moscow Aviation Institute. He was by all accounts the father and scientific pioneer of Soviet UFOlogy, a figure who played a somewhat similar role to that of the late J. Allen Hynek in America. Curiously, the name of Dr. Hynek appears in connection with this photo in one of the many rumors regarding its origin. All sources agree, however, that the photo did indeed come from the files of Prof. Zigel.

As for Marina Popovich, she is a famous test pilot with the rank of full Colonel (Ret.) in the Soviet Air Force, formerly married to the cosmonaut, space hero and member of various official UFO commissions, Air Force General Pavel Popovich. Marina is also the Chairman of the World Association of Women Scientists and President of SACK-UFON, the United UFO Organization of Middle Asia and Kazakhstan. This author finally caught up with her in Tokyo in November of 1990, following her attendance at the International Space & UFO Symposium in Hakui City, Japan. I shall come back later on to her statements about the alien photograph; let's trace first the photo's known history.

The author received the photo confidentially from a well-known American UFOlogist in mid-1990, at which time I was asked to help investigate its authenticity with my Russian sources while keeping the matter quiet. This we did for a while. The story then was that the alien depicted was one of those retrieved in the Roswell of St. Augustine UFO crash of 1947, which somehow came to the hands of Dr. Zigel. Yet the most controversial ingredient was that Zigel had supposedly received the photo from none other than Dr. J. Allen Hynek, the Northwestern University astronomer who was long-time scientific advisor to Project Blue Book and later founded the Center for UFO Studies (CUFOS).

If true, the Hynek connection was explosive stuff, as he was never particularly forthcoming with regards to the subject of crashed saucers. Yet knowledge of Hynek's overt (Blue Book) and possibly covert ties with the U.S. Govern-

ment, have been rumored for long within certain American and foreign UFO circles. Those who knew him closely will at least concede that the good doctor knew far more UFO secrets than what he was willing to tell the public in his numerous lectures, interviews, articles and books.

Subsequently, this author received the same photo from Major (Ret.) Colman von Keviczky, director of ICUFON in New York City, who had obtained it from Michael Hessemann in Germany, together with a brief report of its alleged origin. According to the information supplied by von Keviczky, "at the beginning of 1970, the late Prof. Felix Yurevich Zigel was the head of a Soviet delegation invited to Canada to participate in a high secret conference of American and Canadian governmental scientists. Among other subjects on the conference agenda, the result of the investigation of the [1947] crashed spacecraft and its dead crew members was discussed."

"During the conference," continued von Keviczky's report, "the head of the American delegation loaned to Prof. Zigel the enclosed photographs for special studies." Copies of the photos were later given by Zigel to Marina Popovich. A second photo showing the full body of the humanoid wearing a space uniform stretched over a table, was also enclosed. However, it is such a grainy reproduction which has undergone so many photocopying, that very little original detail can be discerned."

The information was explosive and its repercussions were profound if the story could be validated. After all, we were talking of a top secret conference of American, Canadian and Soviet scientists, where UFOs had been discussed in general and crash/retrievals in particular. Was Hynek the head of the American delegation, who "loaned" confidentially the photos to his Soviet counterpart? And if so, did he have the clearance to do such a thing? Although this could be great news for all the UFO conspiracy buffs, it soon became evident that the Canadian conference had more than a few holes.

For starters, there was no record that Prof. Zigel had ever visited Canada or even gone beyond the borders of the Soviet Union. He had operated in the long days before 'glasnost,' when his UFO research had to be pursued as a hobby which enjoyed no governmental support whatsoever. This was confirmed by Sergei Bulantsev, who was a close friend and colleague of Felix Zigel for some 15 years, and a member of his Moscow UFO group. Bulantsev responded to my inquiries through a friend at the New York office of the Tass News Agency, where he works as Chief of the Foreign Press Bureau. Bulantsev said that "Zigel had never traveled to Canada, that he had never received photos of dead aliens from Hynek or anyone else, and that he had only correspondence with Hynek. This information was 1200 percent correct," according to Bulantsev. But there was still more to the story.

Tracing the origin of unconfirmed rumors like the Canadian conference story, can be tricky stuff; apparently, it did not originate with Marina Popovich. Michael Hessemann confirmed to this author in a letter, which enclosed a yet third copy of the same photo, that "they were presented to me and the Baron von Butlar on the Munich UFO Conference in June 1990 by Col. Dr. Marina Popovich, Soviet Air Force famous test pilot and wife of Gen. Pavel Popovich [now divorced—Ed.]. It will be presented in my 90-minute documentary video *UFO: The Evidence,* where I interviewed Col. Popovich. On the film she has the pictures in her hand, explaining that she got it from the late Prof. Felix Zigel, who got it from Canada, most probably Wilbert Smith."

Here was a new name, in fact, a prominent one when it comes to the matter of crashed saucers retrieved by the U.S. military. The late Dr. Wilbert Smith (1910–62) was a radio engineer who headed for a while Project Magnet, an official Canadian UFO probe in the early 1950s; he was also the author of the classic *The Boys From Topside* (last edition by Inner Light). More importantly, he was the author of the famous "top secret" Department of Transport "Memorandum to the Controller of Telecommunications" of Canada, dated November 21, 1951, which revealed that "the [UFO] matter is the most highly classified subject in the United States Government, a rating higher even than the H-bomb," that "flying saucers exist" and that "their modus operandi is unknown but a concentrated effort is being made by a small group headed by Doctor Vannevar Bush." This memo became one of the crucial pieces of evidence in the affair of the Majestic 12, or MJ-12, documents.

Yet I find it highly unlikely that Wilbert Smith could have been involved with Prof. Zigel. Smith died in 1962, at a time when Zigel was totally unknown in the West. Although his research had begun in 1958, Zigel became only known in 1967, when he appeared on a Moscow TV program with Air Force General Porfiri Stolyarov, urging the audience to submit UFO reports to a short-lived UFO Commission. But even if neither Smith nor Hynek had given Zigel the alien photos, the question of who in Canada had supplied them remained a puzzle.

The reader can see that many allegations—some better founded than others, some contradictory with each other—surround the case. Be that as it may, it appears that Marina Popovich plays a key role in this act, at least for having released the photo to the public. This author had finally a chance of hearing directly her own opinion—rather than a second, third or even a fourth-hand version of it—in Tokyo in late November of 1990. I met Marina at a meeting in Tokyo's UFO Library organized by Kinichi Arai, one of Japan's pioneer UFOlogists. Also present were Dr. Vladimir Azhazha, director of the "Soyuzufosentr" (the All-Union Scientific UFO Coordination Center in Moscow), Dr. Bruce Maccabee of the Fund for UFO Research, Major Colman von Keviczky of ICUFON, and about a dozen Japanese UFOlogists. All had attended the recent International Space & UFO Symposium in Hakui City.

On the following day, November 27, 1990, I interviewed Dr. Azhazha and Col. Marina Popovich at the Washington Hotel in Tokyo's Akihabara electronics district. Since Marina didn't speak any English and Dr. Azhazha knew very little, the taped interview had to be done in Russian, and was later transcribed and translated by Dimitri Ossipov. This is what Marina said regarding the case:

"This photo was given to me long ago by Felix Yurevich Zigel. It was sent to him by a doctor in Canada. Once there was a meeting, there were many pilots and engineers from the Aviation Institute, and he said, 'Go ahead, let's see, I have a photo which was sent to me by a scientist from Canada.' And when extra-sensors—the people who can determine whether this is true or a hoax [i.e., psychics—ed.]—got together, they said that this is a moulding of a real living entity, which perished; it is a molding of a living entity which was photographed."

Marina Popovich then repeated that it was a "moulding of a living entity, not just any moulding. Extra-sensors have checked it. They had a Conference in Muhino, headed by Armstrong, and they all said this is a reproduction of a living entity." When I asked her who had the original photograph, she responded she had a copy of Zigel's but that "the original is in Canada." So Popovich's testimony clarified some aspects, but left others still shrouded in mystery. We can now establish with some degree of certainty that the photo did indeed originate with Prof. Zigel and that he received it long ago from a doctor in Canada.

Secondly, it would appear that the photo "was" shown in a conference with scientists and pilots that took place at the Moscow Aviation Institute, where Zigel taught for many years, but that he never attended a hush-hush conference in Canada. On the other hand, the identity of the Armstrong mentioned by Marina at the ESP Conference in Muhino is still unknown at this time. The name would lead you to believe that it could be Apollo 11 astronaut Neil Armstrong; yet the fact that it was an ESP or parapsychological conference, would suggest that the astronaut in question was not Neil Armstrong but rather Apollo 14's Ed Mitchell, who is the director of the Institute of Noetic Sciences and one of the world's leading experts on ESP. Marina could have simply confused the two names.

The third crucial point in Marina's testimony is the hypothesis alleging that the alien figure in the photo "is a moulding of a real living entity which perished" and "which was photographed." If correct, this would reconcile the apparent contradiction between real and moulding. Interestingly, this new twist of a living alien which died later seems to fit quite well with some of the new evidence that has surfaced regarding the July 1947 UFO crash in the Plains of St. Augustine.

Witness Gerald Anderson claims to have seen the crashed spacecraft with a crew of four aliens when he was five years old and was with several members of his family collecting stones in that part of New Mexico. According to Anderson's testimony, when the military units reached the area, two of the aliens were dead, one was seriously injured and the fourth was in good condition. Thus, our friend in the photo could be one of those who survived for a while but later perished while in custody. Likewise, Stanton Friedman, a nuclear physicist who is probably the leading expert on the New Mexico crash, commented when I showed him a copy of the *Technika Molodezsi* article that the very large eyelids of the humanoid coincided quite well with eyewitness descriptions he had of "oriental eyes."

A new photo of what undoubtedly looks like the same being has recently surface anonymously among American UFOlogists. Its quality is far superior to that of the Russian print and it looks like a different shot of the same being with the same uniform taken perhaps during the same session. We are presently investigating this case, as well as a third obscure photo of a face which looks like a death mask of what could still be the same "real living entity which perished." The full details will appear in my forthcoming book, *RED SKIES—The Glasnost UFO Files.*

A HISTORY OF CRASH/RETRIEVALS AND THE UFO COVER-UP*

By LeRoy Pea
© PEA Research

GOVERNMENT INVOLVEMENT IN THE UFO COVERUP: CHRONOLOGY
(based on Freedom of Information Act Papers)

Apr. 17, 1897...Aurora, TX: An airship supposedly crashed into Judge Proctor's (nonexistent) windmill and disgorged the mangled body of a little man believed, for unspecified reasons, to hail from the planet Mars. This (supposedly) turned out to be a publicity stunt for the town, whose population and economy were on the decline.

1922...County Donegal, Ireland: Irish Republic Army man, Lawrence Bradley, wrote to the editor of "Watford and West-Hersts Post" magazine (4/30/64) that while he was fighting a scattered rear-guard, mostly in the mountains of Donegal, he came upon a cave with vegetation at the entrance that had been scorched. The only occupants in the cave were the sick and the wounded that had been unable to walk. The six able-bodied soldiers that were looking after them said they had been awakened early pre-dawn by a whirring noise outside of the cave and had fired their rifles in the direction of the noise, thinking that it was an armored car. Suddenly the object retaliated by firing jets of flame at the cave entrance. After near suffocation, the soldiers ran out to see the flame-throwing UFO ascending into the sky. Clearly visible, it was circular in shape and glowing and of a

*This appendix is a small portion of a much more detailed history. Readers wishing the full report, including extensive footnotes and sources, are requested to send a stamped self-addressed envelope for ordering details to: PEA Research, 105 Serra Way, Ste. 176, Milpitas, CA 95035

shiny metal.

Feb. 26, 1942: SECRET MEMO to the President from Chief of Staff, C.G. Marshall stating: UFOs appeared over Los Angeles, CA, yesterday morning. The 37th Brigade (AA) expended 1430 rounds of ammunition against them. No bombs dropped, no casualties among our troops, no planes (UFOs) shot down, no AA or Navy planes were in action.

1944: During WW II, E.L. (initials), serving as Carpenter Mate, A5,B3-C 1st Class, Hqt. Co. 112th Construction Battalion, came across a landed saucer near a wooded ridge, near the beach of Kaneohe, Oahu, Hawaii. Description: 50 ft. diam.; metallic; looked like an igloo; topped with a clear glass dome about a foot high with a gold colored weather vane-like device spinning inside.

Sep. 4, 1946: TOP SECRET MEMO, to Mr. Morgan, from Mr. Lyon stating: 800 reports (of UFOs) have been reported with new ones coming in daily from Sweden. Full details of these reports have been forwarded to Wash., D.C. by our Military and Naval Attaches.

Jan. 1947: W.H. (initials) of Yucca Valley, Calif., while still serving in the U.S. Navy, was on leave with C.C. (initials) who was just out of the U.S. army. While they were looking for desert property to buy they came upon the Papagos Indian Reservation, north of the rugged Superstition Mtns. west of Globe, Arizona. While traveling on a dirt trail, they came upon a group of military personnel guarding a crashed saucer half buried in the sand. Description: Disc-shaped with a domed top;

about 30 ft. diam.; two rings on its outer edge which seemed to have windows between them. There was no evidence of an encampment or heavy equipment.

June 24, 1947: A civilian pilot, Kenneth Arnold, reports seeing 9 flying saucers flying in formation at an altitude of 9200 feet and at almost 1700 mph. He estimated them to be 20 to 25 miles away from him and between 45 to 50 feet long.

July 2, 1947: Magdalene, N.M.: Mr. Barnett sighted a shiny object out in the desert and, upon investigation, came upon a crashed disc-shaped object, 9 meters (30 ft.) across. Later a military truck arrived to supervise the investigation of the crash site. Barnett saw dead bodies strewn about the crash site. They weren't wearing military uniforms, and in fact didn't even look human. Seen from a distance, the bodies had on silvery suits and appeared to be about 3 ft. tall.

July 7, 1947: SECRET operation to recover a crashed saucer in New Mexico 75 miles northwest of Roswell Army Air Base (RAAF). FBI, Dallas, sends teletype to director of FBI stating that a flying saucer crashed this date and was recovered near Roswell, N. M.

July 8, 1947: The Roswell Army Air Force captured a downed flying saucer near Roswell, N.M. according to Maj. Marcel as reported by the *Roswell Daily Record*. Maj. J. A. Marcel was intelligence officer at RAAF at the time.

July 8, 1947: URGENT FBI MEMO from Gen. Roger Ramey concerning "flying disc information": "Maj. Curtan, HQ 8th AF, telephonically advised this office that an object purporting to be a flying disc was recovered near Roswell, this date. Information provided this office because of national interest in case and fact that (certain media sources) attempting to break story of location of disc today....(the recovered disc was) being transported to Wright Field by special plane for examination....Maj. Curtan advised would request Wright Field to advise (FBI) results of examination."

July 10, 1947: FBI MEMO: Gen. George F. Schulgen organizes top scientists to determine if the flying disks are indeed fact and whether or not they are a foreign body mechanically devised and controlled. He desired the assistance of the FBI in locating and questioning the individuals who first sighted the disks. Col. L. R. Forney of MID indicated that it has been established that the flying disks are not the result of any Army or Navy experiments and should be of interest to the FBI.

July 12, 1947: In a declassified statement, Kenneth Arnold points out why the unidentified discs he saw couldn't have been mirages: "I observed these objects not only through the glass of my airplane but turned my airplane sideways where I could open my window and observe them with a completely unobstructed view (without sunglasses)."

July 15, 1947: MEMO to Mr. Ladd with a handwritten note from J. Edgar Hoover, Director of the FBI stating, "....before agreeing (to the investigation of crashed saucers)....we must insist upon full access to discs recovered. For instance in the Soc. (Socorro, N.M.) case the Army grabbed it and would not let us have it for cursory examination.

July, 1947: Conclusion to an FBI/ARMY INTELLIGENCE REPORT: Based on a detailed study of the Kenneth Arnold case (6/24/47) and 15 other UFO encounters during the first month of the "flying saucer" mystery the conclusion is "this flying saucer situation is not all imaginary or seeing too much in some natural phenomenon. Something is really flying around." (This report was declassified FOIA, 1976.)

Mid July, 1947: In a paper by U.S. Navy Physicist, Dr. Bruce Maccabee, he stated: "...the Air Force knew by the middle of July, 1947 that saucers were real and not manmade...the technology represented by the (recovered) disc...was so far beyond our own that it could not be understood immediately....Therefore it would be necessary to treat the disc as a military secret. This would mean containing all information about it within some small group." [Date of this Navy paper not mentioned.]

Nov. 30, 1947: In a TOP SECRET DOCUMENT, Dr. Bronk's scientific team classifies extraterrestrials as EBE's (Extra Biological Entities). Sept. 19, 1947... The recovered crashed saucer in New Mexico is determined to be a short range reconnaissance craft (from a mother ship).

Sept. 23, 1947: SECRET BRIEFING DOCUMENT to Brig. General George Schulgen, from Lt. Gen. Nathan F. Twining (MJ-4), Commanding Officer,

AMC, stating: Flying Saucers are REAL! Concerning "Flying Discs" the phenomenon reported is something real, not fictitious. These objects approximate the shape of a disc and appear to be as large as man-made aircraft. They have operating characteristics such as extreme rate of climb and maneuverability. Under a Security Code Name copies of this information will be sent to Army, Navy, AEC, JRDB, SAG, NACA, RAND and NEPA Projects.

Sept. 24, 1947: A covert operation, MAJESTIC-12, is established and classified TOP SECRET by President H. Truman. It consists of 12 persons selected to control all branches of government, both military and non-military. This ultimately led to silencing of UFO witnesses, confiscating of UFO photos, harassing and debunking of witnesses.

Dec. 30, 1947: Project SIGN formed to obtain information about saucer performance characteristics and their purpose on earth.

1948: Capt. Edward J. Ruppelt stated: "With the Soviets practically eliminated as a UFO source the idea of interplanetary spaceships was becoming more popular." [Exact date of statement not mentioned.]

Jan. 7, 1948....Maysville, KN: The local Highway Patrol are notified that a UFO has been sighted high up in the sky and they notify Godman AFB of the sighting....At 1:45 pm T. Sgt. Quinton Blackwell visually scanned the skies south of Godman AFB and picked out a dim light in the hazy sky. By the time base commander Col. Guy Hix arrived at 2:20 pm the UFO looked like "an ice cream cone" through binoculars. About 20 minutes later 4 National Guard aircraft flew into the vicinity with Capt. Thomas Mantell in one of the F-51s.

Jan. 7, 1948: Capt. Thomas Mantell, a Nat. Guard pilot, was killed trying to chase a UFO up to 30,000 ft. His last message to the tower was, "it appears to be metallic object...of tremendous size...directly ahead and slightly above...I am trying to close for a better look." (The F-51 exploded in mid-air and disintegrated before it struck the ground. State Police estimated the saucer to be 250 ft. diam.)

Feb. 13, 1948...Crash/Recovery at Aztec, N.M.: Dr. Gee (actually GeBauer) claimed to have been with the recovery team when 16 little human-like beings were found dead aboard a crashed saucer in N.M. According to Jerome Clark, Gebauer and Silas Newcomb were later arrested for trying to sell "worthless" UFO hardware. (No release date from prison?)

Mar. 25, 1948: The Army OSI and the IPU put on Red Alert and the ADC activated the local military units when a UFO crashed in the vicinity of Aztec, N.M. When the saucer got into range of a Special High-Powered radar at the Four Corners Range (Utah, Arizona, New Mexico, Colorado) it began to flutter and wobble from side-to-side and took a trajectory towards the ground. It seems that the beam from this special radar had an ill-effect on the control system of the saucer. The 100 ft. saucer crash-landed on Mr. H.D.'s property. H.D. and family were sworn to secrecy.

1948: Capt. "Posty" Postlethwaite of G-2 Air, cleared for Top Secret, received a TOP SECRET message incoming from 3rd Army Headquarters, Atlanta, directed to the Commanding General, White Sands Proving Grounds. Message: Crash of a 100 ft. diam. saucer, 30 ft. ht.; one portal window blown; 5 Aliens suffocated; each Alien approx. 4 ft. in ht., oversized heads; hull of craft paper-thin but impenetrable by conventional tools. Private property purchased to facilitate movement of recovered disc.

June 15, 1948: Mr. Booneville observed a reddish glow with a jet exhaust in the vicinity of Miles City, Montana. Made no sound, travelled at twice the speed of conventional aircraft.

July 1, 1948: Maj. Hammer, Rapid City Air Base, reported seeing 12 disks over the base. These disks were oval-shaped and about 100 ft. diam., speed in excess of 500 mph. Made 30 and 40 degree climbing turn, accelerating very rapidly out of sight.

July 17, 1948: Kirtland AFB reported 7 UFOs flying a "J" formation in the vicinity of San Acacia, N.M., at altitude of 20,000 ft. Formation varied from "J" to "L" to "O" after passing zenith. Est. speed 1500 mph.

July 25, 1948: Two Eastern Airlines pilots reported seeing an object like a huge V-2 Rocket pass their jet. Sighted 4 times through scattered clouds and unlimited visibility, travelling at high speed and high altitude. Description: Appeared wingless, had two decks, and made a sound similar to that of a V-2.

Aug. 3, 1948: UFO sighted over Moscow that is similar to the UFO sighted on July 25, 1948, by two Eastern Airlines pilots.

Sept. 12, 1948: Pilot and Co-pilot of a Pan Am aircraft en route from Midway to Honolulu, saw a blue-white light approaching, changing to twin reddish glows upon withdrawal. Est. speed: 1000 knots.

Oct. 1, 1948: 2nd Lt. George F. Gorman (North Dakota Air Nat. Guard), sighted a UFO 3000 ft. below him while he was flying his F-51 at 4500 ft. The pilot pursued the UFO which took evasive tactics. The UFO out-turned, out-speeded and out-climbed the F-51 in every attempt at intercept. The pilot lost contact with the UFO.

Oct. 15, 1948...JAPAN: An F-61 "Black Widow" fighter tracked a UFO on radar and tried to intercept it 6 times without success. It would speed up from 200 mph to 1200 mph, leaving the interceptor behind. Description: shaped like a rifle bullet and apparently 20 to 30 feet long.

Nov. 18, 1948: Report from Project SIGN, incident No. 207 in Blue Book files: at approx. 2200 hours, Lt. Henry G. Combs (AFRes) spotted an oval shaped UFO while flying in a T-6 plane. The UFO accelerated rapidly from 80 mph to 500 or 600 mph. It remained under observation for some 10 minutes. The UFO displayed "evasive controlled tactics and an ability to perform tight circles, quick variation of air speed, vertical ascents and evasive movements." This occurred over Andrews AFB.

Nov. 23, 1948...Wire Report from GERMANY to Project SIGN: Capt. (blank) is an experienced pilot and completely reliable. While flying an F-80 over a US Air Base in the Fursten-Feldbruck area of Germany, he had radar and visual contact with a circling red-lighted UFO at 2200 hours at 27,000 ft. Ground Project SIGN radar determined that it was going 900 mph and climbed quickly to 50,000 ft. in a matter of minutes and disappeared.

Dec. 10, 1948: TOP SECRET Air Intelligence REPORT No. 100-203-79 issued.

Dec., 1948: Project SIGN evolves into Project

GRUDGE and is conducted under the code name BLUE BOOK. The liaison between Project GRUDGE and MJ-12 is Project BLUE BOOK. The Air Force officer is head of BLUE BOOK.

Jan. 6, 1949: Rocket shaped UFO sighted near Los Alamos, N.M.

Jan. 13, 1949: CONFIDENTIAL 4th Army Col. Eustis L. Poland stated: "Unconventional Aircraft" have been sighted. Possible Radiological warfare tests are being made over sensitive Bases in New Mexico area. A foreign power may be making "sensing shots" with some super-stratosphere device designed to be self-disintegrating.

Jan. 31, 1949: CONFIDENTIAL Army Staff MESSAGE: Approx. 30 people sighted UFOs on Jan. 30, 1949. Estimate at least 100 total sightings. Sightings reported from El Paso, Albuquerque, Alamogordo, Roswell, Socorro, and other locations. All sightings appear to be of the same object viewed from possible CRASH different angles. Will attempt to locate the impact point, if any.

Jan. 31, 1949...MEMO, DIRECTOR OF FBI: Flying Saucers have been discussed by the OSI, FBI and the Fourth ARMY and is "considered TOP SECRET by Intelligence Officers of both the Army and the Air Forces." It was thought that the first AEC UFOs over Sweden were of Russian origin. MEMO also makes reference to the Eastern Airlines sighting of July 25, 1948. Also, on 10 different days, between 12/05/48 and 01/06/49, sightings of UFOs were concentrated over B1-G,30 the A.E.C. plant at Los Alamos, N.M. (Circulation of this MEMO to: El Paso, Little Rock, Dallas, Oklahoma City.)

Feb. 4, 1949: CONFIDENTIAL Army Staff MESSAGE dated Jan. 31, 1949 read by OSI: "all out investigation" of possible crashed saucer, OK'd.

Feb., 1949: Part of the Final Report of Project SIGN, written by Prof. George Valley, of MIT stating: "If there is an extraterrestrial civilization which can make objects as are reported, then it is most probable that its development is far in advance of ours...such a civilization might observe that on earth we now have atomic bombs and are fast developing rockets. In view of the past history of mankind, they would be alarmed. We should, therefore, expect at this time above all to behold such visitations."

Apr. 24, 1949...Arrey, NM: Aerologist Charles B. Moore, Jr., while tracking a weather balloon for General Mills Co. with a theodolite suddenly noticed a UFO rapidly crossing the sky. He and 4 other technicians turned the 25 power theodolite to track the UFO. It was a featureless ellipse, its length about 2½ times its width. After about 60 seconds the object disappeared in a sharp climb. Based on measurements with the mountain range behind it, it was calculated to be going between 18,000 mph and 25,000 mph!

May 22, 1949: Secretary Forrestal (MJ-3) is found dead after falling 16 floors from an insane asylum window. [He was supposedly shouting, "we're being invaded!" before he fell to his death.]

June 10, 1949...White Sands, NM: Scientists tracking a test missile at 2,000 ft/second suddenly picked up two small circular UFOs that paced the missile. One of the UFOs passed thru the missiles exhaust and rejoined the other UFO, and together they quickly accelerated upwards leaving the missile behind. Cmdr. McLaughlin received reports from 5 observation posts: ALL had witnessed the performance of the 2 circular UFOs.

Jan. 16, 1950: CLASSIFIED USAF Staff Message: At a radar station near New Mexico a person reported seeing two saucers. One was badly damaged the other almost perfectly intact. Description: Each consisted of 2 parts, a cockpit or cabin about 6 ft. diam.; a ring approx. 18 ft. across and 2 ft. thick surrounding cabin, resembling aluminum, but actual metal has defied analysis by the Dearborne Plant. 2 crew members in the damaged ship were charred but in the undamaged ship the 2 crew members were perfectly preserved.

Jan. 22, 1950...Kodiak, Alaska: U.S. Navy patrol plane pilot, Lt. Smith, was on routine security flight when he picked up a radar track on an UFO, two times. Smith then radioed Kodiak radar station and was advised that no known traffic was in his radar area. Moored south of Kodiak was the USS Tillamock with Master Morgan standing on watch. Suddenly, at 3 A.M., "a very fast moving red glow appeared to be of exhaust nature, seemed to come from the south-east, moved clockwise in a large circle in the direction of, and around Kodiak and returned out in a generally south-east direc-

tion. The UFO was moving so fast that it was actually leaving a streak on Smith's radar screen. It was estimated to be moving at a speed of 1800 mph. Described as "two orange lights rotating about a common centre like two jet aircraft making slow rolls in tight formation." The UFO then made an abrupt turn and headed directly towards Smith's aircraft in a threatening gesture so Smith quickly turned off all of his lights turn make his plane less conspicuous in the inky colored sky. The UFO flew by him and disappeared in the south-east in a matter of minutes.

Jan. 31, 1950: Office MEMO, Director FBI, SAC, San Antonio: A UFO resembling a rocket ship without wings appeared out of a thunderhead of clouds narrowly missing an Eastern Airlines flight and disappeared into another cloud. It was travelling approx. 2700 mph and no sound or air disturbance was noted with it. During the past two months the UFO sightings appeared to be concentrated near Los Alamos, N.M. This UFO was also sighted near Los Alamos on Jan. 6, 1949.

Mar. 22, 1950...FBI MEMO: 3 saucers recovered in New Mexico. Description: Circular with raised centers, approx. 50 ft. diam. Each one occupied by 3 bodies, only 3 ft. tall, dressed in metallic suit, tapered like high-speed flyers. It is believed that a very high powered Radar Station interfered with their control mechanisms, causing them to crash.

Mar. 22, 1950: Dept. Transportation, Ottawa, Canada, announces plans to build and test free energy geomagnetic engine. Also state that "Dr. Vannevar Bush heads Highest Secret saucer research group in the U.S.A.".

Mar. 31, 1950: MEMO to Director, F.B.I. pertaining to flying saucers. Memo names a person in Denver, Colorado that claims to possess a UFO radio transmitter.

Aug. 1, 1950: Gen. Walter B. Smith fills the vacant MJ-3 position of the late Secretary Forrestal.

Aug. 4, 1950: CONFIDENTIAL MEMO from Lt. Colonel Mildren (G-3) to Maj. Carlan (GSC Survey Section): Since July 30, 1950, UFOs have been sighted over the Hanford AEC Plant. Air Force jets failed to intercept them. FBI, anti-aircraft battalion, radar units and fighter squadrons alerted for further observation. Atomic Energy Commission still investigating.

Sep.15, 1950: Notes from a conference between Canadian, Wilbert Smith, and Dr. Robert Sarbacher, scientist reveals: Frank Sculley's book, *Behind the Flying Saucers* is true and substantially correct. Flying Saucers do exist. The Government hasn't been able to duplicate their performance. It's pretty certain they don't originate on the earth. The subject is the highest classified SECRET in the United States; two points higher than H-bomb research.

Oct. 6, 1950: CONFIDENTIAL MEMO, Headquarters, 5th Army Division: John de Reneaux photographed the saucer which crashed near Aztec, N.M. He said that "army officials" had attempted to take the photographs away from him but that he had given them another roll of film. In a further interview with the 5th Headquarters, de Reneaux denied any knowledge of the Aztec crash.

Dec. 6, 1950: A second flying saucer crashes in El Indio-Guerrero area. The saucer is recovered and taken to the AEC facility at Sandia, N. M. 1950s, late...The so-called Interplanetary Phenomenon Unit (IPU) was disestablished and all records were transferred to the Air Force.

Feb. 10, 1951: CONFIDENTIAL MEMO to Air Transport Squadron ONE: Lt. Graham E. Bethune, U.S. Naval Reserve reported seeing a circular, reddish-orange UFO flying at a speed in excess of 1000 mph, approx. 300 ft. diam. approaching ICELAND and reversing direction within 5 miles of his plane (Flight 125 from Keflavik, Iceland.)

July 9, 1951: Pilot Lt. Kinmon sees and reports a UFO.

July 10, 1951: CLASSIFIED OSI Message from Robins AFB, Macon: UFO sighted by Lt. George H. Kinmon Jr. on July 9, 1951. Description: Flat on top and bottom and appeared from front view to have rounded edges, slightly beveled. Color was white. When it dived from its position it appeared circular with a clockwise spinning motion. Appeared to have a cratered surface. No exhaust fumes or visible means of propulsion. At an approx. distance from his plane the UFO appeared to be 10 to 15 feet in diam. UFO caused air disturbance as it barrel-rolled under his plane. His nose camera malfunctioned.

Sep. 10, 1951: CONFIDENTIAL Air Intell. REPORT: Maj. Ballard and Lt. Rogers while flying at 20,000 ft. in a T-33 spotted a disc-shaped UFO the size of an F-86 flying below them at 8000 ft. It was travelling much faster than they were (900+ mph). It was steady in flight, with no visible means of propulsion and shiny silver in color. The radar station at Ft. Monmouth plotted the same UFO on radar at 1110 EDT flying above 700 mph.

Oct., 1951: Project GRUDGE is on hold, Intelligence Officer Capt. Edward J. Ruppelt has been assigned to reshape the study and field mounting concern for the Pentagon.

Oct. 21, 1951: Air Intelligence Report: Mr. (name withheld), a civilian pilot of 14 years experience sighted a disk-like, highly polished UFO which closed head on with his Navion aircraft at an extremely high rate of speed near Battle Creek, MI. [Missed him, I guess!]

March, 1952: Capt. Edward J. Ruppelt recommends a new name for Project Grudge, "Project Blue Book".

Apr 25, 1952: UFO sighted flying over San Jose, CA, near Mt. Hamilton by two scientists, Dr. W (biochemist; name withheld) and Dr. Y (bacteriologist, name also withheld). Description of hovering disk: at about 50 ft. it appeared to be 4 to 5 ft. in diam. The wobble of the disk allowed them to estimate its thickness to be approx. 1.5 ft. No sound or means of propulsion observed. Later they observed a higher flying silvery disc approx. 100 ft. in diam. Next more UFOs appeared and bobbed around like boats in a stream. The objects disappeared around 11:15 A.M. The two scientists decided not to report the incident to Moffett Field for fear of ridicule.

1952?: SECRET SECURITY INFORMATION, CIA, (not dated): Walter B. Smith, Director of CIA notifies the Psychological Strategy Board that "Flying Saucers" have implications for psychological warfare as well as for intelligence and operations. Suggests discussion on the possible PSYCHOLOGICAL WARFARE offensive or defensive utilization of these phenomena for psychological warfare purposes.

May 10, 1952: RESTRICTED USAF Intelligence Report signed by Col. William L. Travis, Chief USAF Intelligence Div. stating: at 2030 hours, in the city of Paphos, S.W. Cypress, a group of persons including a noted British Scientist sighted an UFO which appeared to rise sharply from the level of the sea and disappeared into the sky. It was of a circular shape and emitted a luminous light. It appeared to waver back and forth before fading out of sight directly overhead.

June 4, 1952: RESTRICTED USAF Intelligence Report. While Operation INTERCEPT was in effect, two North American Sabre fighters were vectored onto a target UFO. The pilots had a broad daylight view of the UFO and fired tracer bullets at it before it accelerated out of range. The officer who fired the bullets was debriefed by his Colonel (name withheld) and the base commander told Capt. Ruppelt to destroy the report (according to Ruppelt himself).

July 19, 1952: Washington, D.C.: Long range "overfly" RADAR picked up a formation of seven blips that were 15 miles south and not far from Andrews AFB. Radar operator, Ed Nugent, thought that they were military traffic until two of (see Movie: *Earth vs. the Flying Saucers*) the targets suddenly accelerated at fantastic speeds and disappeared off the radar scope. These strange UFOs were monitored by Harry Barnes, Senior Controller, and controllers Howard Cocklin and Joe Zacko. Also, Andrews AFB had also been tracking the UFOs as they intruded over the White House which was restricted air space. The UFOs were traveling at speeds of up to 7000 mph. UFOs "Show Superiority" before stopping abruptly and then cruising about in unconventional patterns.

July 20, 1952: CLASSIFIED SPOT INTELLIGENCE REPORT (dated 7/23/52): 3 UFO spotted by 5 base personnel at Andrews AFB at 0030 hours EST. UFOs reddish orange in color, moving erratically at an undetermined altitude. Approach Control picked up another UFO at 0415 EST which was on the radar scope for 30 seconds before fading. Lt. Hyatt, Operations Officer during this period, said that he had been receiving "flying saucer" reports that evening and the objects had been picked up by radar.

July 23, 1952: In a letter to a Mr. Louis A. Gardner, Albert Einstein said with regards to UFOs, "those

people have seen something. What they saw I do not know and I am not curious to know."

July 26, 1952: Washington, D.C.: Long range "overfly" RADAR picks more blips, just one week after the previous invasion of restricted air space over Washington, D.C. Capt. Ruppelt told Maj. Dewey Fournet to get over to the airport in Washington. Fournet was a radar specialist with Project HOLCOMBE and arrived at the airport with Al Chop, AF Press Officer, just in time to see the UFO blips on the radar sets and to hear ground-to-air conversations of the pilots of two F-94s vectored towards the UFOs.

July 28, 1952: Personal Memo from Prime Minister W.S. Churchill to Secretary of Air Ministry stating: "What does all this stuff about Flying Saucers amount to? What can it mean? What is the truth? Let me have a report at your convenience."

July 29, 1952: SECRET, EYES ONLY MEMO to Deputy Director/Intelligence from Ralph L. Clark, Acting Assistant Director of Scientific Intelligence stating: In the past several weeks numerous UFOs have been sighted visually and on SPECIAL UFO GROUP RADAR. This office (CIA) has maintained a continuing review of reputed sightings for the past three years and a SPECIAL GROUP has been formed to review the sightings to date. OCI and OSI will participate in this study and prepare a report on UFOs by August 15, 1952.

End of July: *OPERATION INTERCEPT*: 1952... SECRET MEMO to Director, CIA, from H. Marshall Chadwell, Office of Scientific Intelligence stating: ATIC has set up a worldwide reporting network for Flying Saucers and major Air Force bases have been ordered to make INTERCEPTIONS of UFOs. Battello Memorial Institute is to handle machine indexing of all official reported sightings. From 1947 to date, there have been 1500 official sightings with 250 of them in 1952 alone. Of the 1500, 28% remain UNEXPLAINED. UFOs are of such importance that the matter should be brought before the National Security Council.

Aug. 1, 1952: CIA MEMO from acting Chief of Weapons and Equipment Division: "It is strongly urged, however, that no indication of CIA interest or concern by CIA reach the press or public."

Aug. 9, 1952: Reply from Air Ministry, Whitehall,

S.W. to W.S. Churchill stating: All UFO sightings are either astronomical phenomena, mistaken sightings of balloons, birds, etc., optical illusions or hoaxes. The Americans have reached a similar conclusion.

Aug. 16, 1952: CIA analysis report of a Vienna news article of a UFO report from the Belgian Congo: Commander Pierre of Elisabethville Airfield was sent out to intercept two Flying Saucers. They had a diam. of 12 to 15 meters with a stationary central hub with visible portholes and an extremely fast rotating outer disk that glowed as if on fire. Color similar to aluminum. They emitted a loud whistling sound which could be heard over his own engines. He estimated their speed at over 1500 kilometers/hour.

Aug. 20, 1952: Memorandum for Director CIA: the DCI, after a briefing by OSI on the subject of UFOs, directed the preparation of an NSCID for submission to the Council stating the need for investigation and directing agencies concerned to cooperate in such investigations. It was decided that Dr. Whitman, chairman of P&DB, would investigate undertaking R&D studies through Air Force agencies. Signed: H. Marshall Chadwell.

Aug. 23, 1952: CIA analysis report of an Athens news article of an UFO landing in Communist Berlin, Germany: Former Mayor of Gleimershausen, Oscar Linke and his 11 year old daughter, Gabriella, spotted a landed Flying Saucer near the town of Hasselbach. The huge "frying pan" was approx. 13 to 15 meters in diameter and had two rows of holes on its periphery, about 30 centimeters in circumference. The space between the two rows was about 0.45 meters. On top was a black conical object about 3 meters high. Two men dressed in shiny metallic clothing were standing outside the craft. Upon hearing the daughter's voice the two men retreated into the UFO which then began to rotate. As the UFO began to spin the conical tower slid down into the UFO and the UFO began to rise and rotate like a top. It seemed to be supported by the conical tower that was now underneath it. (more details were included in report)

Sep. 19, 1952...Air Ministry, London: A number of airmen and officers of the R.F, Topcliffe, observed an UFO. As it descended it was swinging in a pendular motion like a falling leaf. Pendulous motion ceased and object began rotary motion about its own axis. Suddenly accelerated at an incredible speed. It was not identifiable with any known aircraft and acceleration was in excess of that of a shooting star! Craft was silver in color and circular.

Sep. 20, 1952: An UFO similar to the Topcliffe one is sighted over a U.S. Carrier ship out with the fleet between England and Scandinavia. An American photographer doing a story of the fleet exercise took pictures of the UFO which was ascertained not to have been a balloon. The Navy never released the photos of the UFO.

Sep. 21, 1952: Six RAF jets on maneuvers over the North Sea saw a "sphere" heading towards them, coming from the direction of the English fleet. It was tracked on radar then disappeared and reappeared behind them. One Meteor pilot attempted an intercept but was completely outrun by the UFO. Capt. Ruppelt was later told by RAF Intelligence that the incidents of the past three days caused the RAF to officially recognize the UFO situation.

Oct. 2, 1952: SECRET MEMO to Director CIA from H. Marshall Chadwell, Assistant Director of Scientific Intelligence: ATIC is the only group devoting appreciable effort to the study of UFOs. Flying Saucers pose two elements of danger to the United States. The first involves mass psychological considerations and the second concerns vulnerability of the U.S. to air attack. Recommend that the DCI discuss this subject with the Psychological Strategy Board.

Oct. 27, 1952: Air Intelligence MEMO: "Some military officials are seriously considering the possibility of (UFOs being) interplanetary ships."

Nov. 18, 1952: MAJESTIC-12 briefing document to President (elect) Eisenhower from Admiral R. Hillenkoetter (MJ-1).

Nov. 25, 1952: (cont'd briefing from 8/20/52): Memorandum for Director CIA: Another meeting by A-2 and ATIC personnel was held on this date. UFOs must have immediate attention. UFOs have been sighted at great altitude and at high speeds in the vicinity of major U.S. defense installations and can NOT be attributed to natural phenomena or KNOWN types of aerial vehicles. OSI is proceeding to establish an immediate PRIORITY research and development on UFOs under the aegis of CANIS. Signed: H. Marshall Chadwell.

Dec. 2, 1952: Statement by H. Marshall Chadwell, Assistant Director of Scientific Intelligence, CIA: "The reports of (UFO) incidents convince us that there is UFOs: something going on that must have immediate attention."

1953: Director of Project Blue Book, Capt. Ruppelt stated: "Two RAF Intelligence Officers who were in the U.S. on a classified mission brought six single-spaced typed pages of questions they and their friends wanted answered regarding UFOs.

1953?: Pilot (name withheld) stated, "a saucer crashed in a desert area". He was sure that it was just inside the Arizona border. He also saw the bodies first-hand at Wright-Patterson AFB. The crates arrived at night by DC-7. Description of bodies: approx. 4 ft. ht. Resting unshrouded on special blanket on dry ice. Heads were hairless, narrow, disproportionately large for their bodies. Skin had brown tint. Open eyes, small mouth, indistinct nose, hands and feet. Wore tight fitting, dark colored suites. One alien appeared to be female. One alien had been alive at the crash sight but attempts to save its life with oxygen failed.

Jan., 1953: The ROBERTSON PANEL convenes, headed by Prof. H.P. Robertson. He was chosen because of being renowned as a nuclear physicist. Some of the persons involved with this panel were Capt. Ruppelt, Dr. Allen Hynek, Prof. S. Sam Goudsmit, Prof. Luis Alvarez, Dr. Lloyd Berkner and Prof. Thornton Page.

Jan. 26, 1953: The Dept. of Defense, Washington, D.C. states in a letter to Henry Holt & Co. that Maj. Donald Keyhoe's book on flying saucers is accurate and that if the reported controlled maneuvers of the saucers are accurate then the saucers may be from another planet. Signed, Albert M. Chop, Air Force Press Desk.

May 21, 1953...Kingman, Ariz.: Fritz Werner (pseudonym), engineer at Wright-Patterson AFB, assisted in the investigation of a crashed UFO. It was constructed of an unfamiliar metal, similar to aluminum [magnesium?]. It had impacted 20 inches into the sand without any signs of structural damage. It was oval and 30 ft. in diam. An opened hatchway was 3½ ft. long and ½ ft. wide. Inside the craft were 2 swivel seats, oval cabin and lots of instrumentation and displays. A tent pitched nearby contained the corpse of the pilot. It was approx. 4 ft. tall and had a brown complexion, two eyes, a small round mouth, two nostrils [no nose?], and two ears. It wore a silvery metallic-like suit and a skull cap of the same material.

Summer, 1953: Saucer crash lands near Camp Polk, Louisiana. US Army Prvt. H.J. (initials) under Sgt. R.S. (initials) in Company B ordered to stay by saucer until ambulance and superior officers arrive. Three aliens walked away from the crash. One Alien was carried on a stretcher. All aliens eventually died, taken to storage facility near Washington D.C. Alien description: Large helmeted heads, tight fitting suits, legs stiff when they walked, 3.5 to 4.0 feet tall, used alien language.

June 24, 1953: USAF EMERGENCY Intelligence Report: Two jets out of Quonset Point have had mid-air collision at 2130E with UFO. American and Eastern Airlines pilots reported UFO. Jets fell in flames 15 miles West of Quonset Point.

June 26, 1953: USAF Intelligence Report, EMERGENCY JEDUP JEDEN JEDFF JEPHQ JEPRS 555. Distribution: OOP, OOP-CP, OAC, ARMY, NAVY, JCS, CIA, NSA, Tech Intelligence Center Wright Patterson AFB.

July 19, 1953: CONFIDENTIAL Message to the Adjutant General, Wash. 25 D.C.: An F-86 aircraft was observed in flight over the Oak Ridge residential area by a writer and his wife. While observing the F-86 thru 6 power field glasses an UFO, black in color, moved out of a high white cloud directly over the area where the F-86 had been circling. The UFO began circling at a tremendous speed for at least 5 minutes. It appeared at times to be cigar shaped and at other times to be round in shape. No sound or visible means of propulsion was observed from the UFO. It flew away at tremendous speed for 3 miles where it was joined by 2 other UFOs into a 'V' formation and sped away.

July 26, 1953: EMERGENCY message to Air Defense Command: sighted 7 UFOs hovering at altitude of 5 to 8 thousand feet near Perrin Tower, TX. Visually observed by citizens of Denison and Sherman, TX. The UFOs were grouped in a Z (Zebra) formation, then circled to higher altitude and faded from sight. Each UFO had one bright red light on it.

July 27, 1953: SECURITY INFORMATION, CONFIDENTIAL message to Adjutant General, Wash. 25 D.C.

Aug. 26, 1953: Regulation AFR 200-2 issued to Air Force personnel for reporting UFOs.

Nov. 2, 1953: Changes updated for UFO reporting. New Regulation AFR 200-2A.

1953: Project xxxxxx (name CENSURED) established by President Eisenhower and renamed Project AQUARIUS (1960).

Winter, 1953: Salisbury Plain, England: Flight Lt. C.G. Townsend-Withers was flying an experimental Canberra aircraft at 55,000 ft. when he picked up on the new experimental radar an UFO following his plane. The science officer went up to the turret for a visual and spotted a circular craft five miles behind them. They tried to outpace the UFO by accelerating to 225 knots but it kept up with their plane. Townsend-Withers initiated a wide sweeping turn and lost radar contact with the UFO but came into direct visual on a collision course with the UFO. Then the UFO flipped vertically in the air and climbed from 50 to 70 thousand feet, as quickly as you could say it. Desc.: Round, thin disc with two tailfins at the rear, appearing metallic and enormous. Leaving no vapor trail, wake or detectable sound, it vanished within a couple of seconds up into the blue sky.

Dec. 8, 1953: CIA Evaluation of the UFO situation: It was pleased to note that the number of sightings had decreased dramatically, due, it believed, to the success of its' implemented policies. Some sightings still would have "possible scientific intelligence value". The CIA concluded that the panel's (name?) recommendations might have been interpreted by saucer believers as "debunking".

Feb. 6, 1954: CONFIDENTIAL Air Force Staff MESSAGE: From Commander, A-Division, Carswell AFB, TX,: UFO sighted over base. Had long fuselage, elliptical wings, stabilizer and no visible means of propulsion. It was larger than a B-36, had no tail, left no trail of exhaust and emitted no sound. Passed directly over tower at an Alt. of 3000 to 4000 ft. and was visible to all persons on duty.

UFO, when viewed on 10 mile scope gave a return of 1 inch. Copy of this report sent to: CSAF, WASH DC; COMDR ADC, ENT AFB, COLO; COMDR ATINTEL, CRT WPAFB, OHIO; COMDR 8TH AF, CARSWELL AFB, TEX.

Feb. 20, 1954: Supposedly, some people think, President Eisenhower went to see the captured saucers and recovered bodies at Edward Air Force Base Hanger-18, instead (according to his press agent) of being at the dentist. Between 6:30 and 7:15 P.M. a saucer crashed in the desert, near Bandelier, N.M. K.A. (initials) and Rescue Team 4 were sent from Roswell AFB to A5 investigate the crashed disc. The saucer was 40–50 ft. in diameter. There were 4 dead Aliens scattered about the desert by the saucer. Alien description (seen from helicopter at 30 ft. alt.): Height was between 4.0 to 4.5 ft. Large proportioned heads, no helmets. Tight fitting dark blue suite. Faces, under 'copter spotlight, were light green with a luminous tint. The saucer was stored in Hanger-18, Top Security. Hanger-18 was later expanded to 9 stories high and 11 stories deep with heavy refrigeration equipment, radar equip., and sophisticated computer equip.

Aug. 12, 1954: EMERGENCY CIA MESSAGE: Lighted Saucer hovering at 2000 ft. above Maxwell AFB, Alabama. Dispatched local helicopter to investigate. Definitely NOT a star. Helicopters fuel low, returned to base. Incoming helicopter proceeded toward UFO which then completely disappeared. Pilot lost sight of it, would be glad to be called upon to verify saucer light. Pilots of Army helicopters were: R.T. Wade, 506th helicopter Co., U.S. Tarma, also of the 506th, Ft. Genning, GA.

Aug. 12, 1954: New updated reporting of UFOs. Regulation AFR 200-2, Aug. 26, 1953), by order of N.F. Twining (MJ-4), Chief of Staff, USAF.

1954: Project SIGMA established as part of Project xxxx (name CENSURED). Became a separate project in 1976.

June 29, 1954: A BOAC Strato Cruiser (British Airways) on a trans Atlantic flight with Capt. James Howard in command was traveling at 260 knots at 19,000 ft. when the crew saw a large CIGAR shaped UFO with six smaller UFOs flying close to it. Among the others to witness these events were First Officer Lee Boyd and Navigator Capt. H. McDonnell. After 15 minutes of observing the

UFOs, U.S. Capt. Howard radioed Goose Bay, Canada, for backup escort, upon which the smaller UFOs entered the bigger Cigar shaped one which then shot away. Upon landing, Howard and Boyd were debriefed by intelligence officers and their flight logs were confiscated by USAF personnel.

July 14, 1954: MEMO to General Nathan F. Twining (MJ-4) requesting his presence at a MAJESTIC-12 meeting with President Eisenhower on July 16.

July 16, 1954: SECRET meeting between Gen. Nathan Twining (MJ-4) and President Eisenhower.

Aug., 1954: Statement by Air Chief Marshall Lord Dowding, head of the RAF during WWII: "Of course the flying saucers are real! And, they are interplanetary!"

Oct. 14, 1954: North Weald Airfield, Essex, England: Flight Lt. Jimmy Salandin took off in his Meteor jet at 4:15 pm and climbed up to 16,000 ft. When he was over Southend, England, two circular UFOs shot past him at 9 o'clock high. One UFO was silvery and the other gold in color. A third UFO appeared ahead of him on a collision course. It had a bun-shaped top, a flange like two saucers in the center and a bun shaped dome underneath and was silvery in color. It flew close enough to his jet to overlap his windshield.

Feb. 23, 1955: Broadlands Archives Record: Sworn statement by Lord Mountbatten and Frederick Briggs describing a saucer that landed on Lord Mountbatten's property. It was shaped like a child's humming top, between 10 to 30 ft. diameter. Looked like kitchen saucepan. Had cylindrical column about the size of a man descending from the center. Had portholes all around the middle, like a steamer boat. I noticed a man standing on the end of the central column. He was dressed in a dark suit of overalls, and wearing a close fitting hat or helmet. As the Saucer powered up a bright blue light came from one of the portholes (like a mercury-vapor lamp). A force knocked me over. The flying saucer proceeded to rise and retract the central column."

Mar. 7, 1955: K.A. (initials) from Rescue Team 4, Roswell AFB, N.M. given a general discharge from the USAF because he told his Sergeant about the Top Secret recovery of a UFO on April 12, 1954.

July 12, 1955: Unusual UFOB report from Pepperrel AFB, Newfoundland. UFO sighted by a tanker aircraft (KC 97) pilot and ground radar. "Unusual" in that the pilot of the Archie 29 called direction changes of the UFO to ground radar which correlated exactly with those painted by the radar scope. This observation went on for 49 minutes. Signed: Todos M. Odarenko.

Oct. 9, 1955: General Douglas MacArthur states, "The nations of the world will have to unite—for the next war will be an interplanetary war. The nations of the Earth must someday make a common front against attack by HOSTILE ALIENS people from other planets."

Late 1956: Castle AFB, California: A.A. and J.R. (names withheld) were flying F-86's near Modesto, CA, on alert duty due to civilian UFO reports in a nearby town. Base instructed them to return because their was an UFO near the control tower. With afterburners on they closed rapidly on a luminous elliptical UFO that moved above and below cloud cover at 10 to 12 thousand feet as if to elude them. The two pilots played cat-and-mouse with the UFO until they ran low of fuel and returned to base. Local citizens that witnessed these events were told by the Air Force that the pilots had been chasing ducks or geese.

Aug. 31, 1957: In a letter about UFOs to a constituent, Senator Barry Goldwater said, "I, frankly, feel there is a great deal to this." Oct. 4, 1957... "Sputnik I" was launched and obtained orbit by the Russians.

Nov. 2, 1957...Levelland, TX: Multiple landings on roadways, E-M effects, etc. Sheriff Weir Clem was sent out to search the roads as a result of earlier UFO reports and saw a reddish oval crossing the road and illuminating the pavement. Ronald Martin saw an UFO land in front of his truck and turn from red to bluish-green at which time the truck's electrical system failed. It then turned reddish again and took off. Within the next few hours an Army Jeep Patrol at White Sands, N.M., reported an egg-shaped UFO that descended to about 50 yards above a bunker used during the first A-bomb explosion. This wave of sightings continued for 2–3 weeks. After retirement in 1975, Sheriff W. Clem gave a more graphic description of the UFO he saw: "The object was shaped like a huge football and had bright white lights. No living human could believe how fast it travelled. The thing was as bright as day. It lit up the whole area." In an interview in 1977, Sheriff Clem said, "After the publicity of UFOs over the next few days, the number of witnesses to them rose to about a hundred people."

Nov. 5, 1957: A single investigator from Project Blue Book headquarters arrived at Levelland, TX, and interviewed only two persons who had stalled cars and reported that all the UFO activity in Texas between Nov. 2-4 was the result of a "rather heavy electrical storm...All witnesses saw the same streak of lightning...which stimulated the populace into a high level of excitement...and resulted in an inflation of stories by some witnesses."

Nov. 12, 1957...FBI STATUS REPORT: "Ever since the Russians release 'Sputnik' there has been a great increase in the number of flying saucers and other UFOs reportedly seen by people all over the U.S." [Angle: Artificial satellite spurs Alien interest in mankind. Other Angle: Art. satel. causes populace to go sky crazy.]

Early 1960's: Frank Scully dies. (Author of *Behind the Flying Saucers*.)

1961–1963: Near Nellis AFB, NE: "Mat," a radio maintenance engineer at Nevada's AEC between 1961–1963, provided evidence to the *MUFON Journal* that Project REDLIGHT was secretly being conducted at nearby "Area 51," a 50-mile-square quadrant of land east of Nellis AFB. This Project "involved" flight-testing of a UFO, which had been shipped there from Edwards AFB." The craft flew silently, was about 20 to 30 ft. in diam., and had no wings or tail.

Apr., 1962: Flight Commander P.J. (initials), attached to TAC FighterWing was deployed at Wright-Patterson AFB and mistakenly broke into an air hanger where he thought the gym was located. Upon entering the hanger he was approached by an air police sentry with a submachine gun. Behind the sentry was a saucer approx. 12–15 ft. diam. suspended off the ground by two engine test stands. There were no markings or insignia on the saucer. It had no rivet markings. The saucer was roped-off and 8 guards stood at parade rest around it. P.J. and his friend were encouraged to leave the hanger. P.J. returned to Myrtle Beach AFB, S.C.

1965: While visiting the Air Force Museum in Fairborn, Ohio, R.M. (initials), a government employee of 23 yrs., went through a doubledoor marked "Off Limits" and suddenly came face to face with an alien with blue skin in a self contained space suit. Description: About 4.5 ft. tall with walked Stiff legged. a translucent dome over its' large head; wasn't human; large eyes under a heavy brow; no noticeable nose; a slit for a mouth; bluish skin. When the creature walked it didn't bend its' knees. R.M. later found out from a retired Air Force Colonel from Wright-Patterson AFB, that 2 live Aliens were held in captivity in an artificial environment. The Colonel also said that a 2-man sized craft crashed near Whitewater Lake, Indiana, as a result of an electrical disturbance in the atmosphere.

Nov., 1965...Fort Riley, KA: "AK" (Aaron Kaback) was on guard duty at 2 a.m. when the duty officer drove up and ordered him to hop into the jeep. He and 3 other officers were driven out to a remote area where a large oval object was resting. An army chopper was hovering above the object and shining a bright light on it. The object was approx. 35–48 ft. in diam., had a fin on the end and an exhaust port or some kind of hole below the fin. It had rows of squares around the rim and remained completely dead for the 2½ hours they guarded it. (Kaback seems to be confused as to the actual date this incident occurred.)

Mar. 1, 1967: Lt. Gen. Hewitt T. Wheless, USAF, sends notice to all branches of the military warning of persons imitating military officers and harassing private citizens and confiscating UFO photos.

July 3, 1967: R.T. (initials), with ALPHA RED TOP SECRET CRYPTO Clearance, assigned to Canine Corps at Camp Pendleton, San Diego, CA., states that he and his dogs were air transported 2.5 hrs. to a sight in a desert (unknown location) UFO crash-sight. Saucer: Metallic, 30 ft. diameter, domed top, no windows. Also observed: Large walk-in refrigerator, empty body bags, men at work with technical instruments.

Oct. 1969: Jimmy Carter sees and reports a UFO.

1972: Project SNOWBIRD established to test fly a captured flying saucer.

Sept., 1973: At Great Lakes Naval Base, Instructor R.K., while delivering a sealed envelope to the Commandant in the quonset hut, was surprised to see a saucer 30 ft. diam. and 10 ft. ht. resting on a wooden platform. Description: Silvery blue and shimmering, it tapered like a teardrop with a flange running along its topside from one end to the other and there were no windows. R.K. believed this saucer to be the one shot down on its third pass over a Navy vessel by a missile. The saucer crashed in 350 ft. water between Hawaii and the mainland. It was retrieved by a Glomar Explorer, shipped to Hawaii then stateside to Chicago.

Mar. 28, 1975: Letter from Senator Barry Goldwater stating: "Ten or twelve years ago I tried to get access to the building at Wright-Patterson where UFO artifacts were stored and I was understandably denied access. It is still classified above TOP SECRET. I've heard they plan to release some of the information in the near future and hope not to have to wait too much longer."

Aug. 13, 1975...Alamogordo, NM: Staff Sgt. Charles L. Moody, USAF, drove out to the outskirts of town late one night to watch for meteors. As a disc-shaped UFO descended toward him, he tried to start his car to get away but it wouldn't start. He heard a high pitched whining sound from the UFO and saw shadowy figures in it and felt numbness, after which the UFO departed. After driving home he found he couldn't account for 1.5 hours. The next day his back was inflamed and he discovered a small puncture wound over his spine and a few days later he developed a body rash. As months passed he regained memory of the missing 1.5 hours. He remembered that he had been in the UFO and in telepathic communication with small 4'8" humanoids. They had whitish-gray skin, large heads, large eyes, small slit-like mouths and mask-like features. He had been in a drug-like state on a table and they had poked a rod-like device into his back. After this they escorted him about the ship and later dropped him off at his car.

Sept.16, 1980: Sgt. J.M. (initials) of the PACAF writes to Len Stringfield that he was stationed at McGuire AFB, N.J., when, on Jan. 18, 1978, an MP shot and killed an alien at the Ft. Dix Army base next to the AFB.

December 27–29, 1980: USAF UFO REPORT signed by Lt. Col. Charles I. Halt, Deputy Base Commander, RAF Woodbridge stating: Two USAF security police patrolmen saw a UFO either hovering or on legs outside the back gate, Woodbridge, England. Being early morning, it illuminated the entire forest with a white light. Description: Metallic in appearance and triangular in shape, pulsing red light on top and banks of blue lights underneath. Approx. 2–3 meters across and 2 meters ht. It maneuvered through the tries and disappeared. Witnesses said 5 aliens emerged from craft and seemed to be performing repairs.

Dec. 29, 1980: A low-flying UFO was escorted by a large number of helicopters (23) including some Chinooks and possibly Hueys, near Dayton, Texas. It was probably escorted to the TOP SECRET underground installation within Fort Hood, Texas. The SECRET Air Force Base is NOT listed in the Air Force Officer's Guide or the Air Force Almanac [it is an Army AFB]. The name of the Secret base is Gray AAF, Texas. The special group piloting the helicopters are known as the "BLUE-BOYS." The Texas Department of Public Safety works closely with Gray AAF on UFO cases.

June 24, 1983: Larry W. Bryant, Director of CAUS, filed a Civil Action, (Judge Oliver Gasch) petitioning for a Writ of Habeas Corpus in the United States District Court for the Dist. of Columbia, seeking to obtain the release from custody of "one or more occupants of apparent extraterrestrial origin." Mr. Bryant contends that the Government action in maintaining secret custody, detention, and prosecution of such extraterrestrials is unlawful and a violation of their basic rights and is seeking to restore their civil rights

Nov. 29,1983: Dr. Robert I Sarbacher, President and Chairman of the Board, Washington Institute of Technology, in a letter to William Steinman states persons definitely involved in operations of recovered saucers were John von Neuman and Dr. Vannevar Bush. Also, Dr. Sarbacher thought that Robert Oppenheimer was also involved. Dr. Sarbacher had been invited by President Eisenhower to attend several discussions associated with the reported recoveries, but was unable to attend them. He did receive Special Reports on the recoveries at the Pentagon but was instructed NOT to remove them from his office.

May 16, 1984: Dept. of the Army letter to W. S. Steinman stating that the IPU was disestablished in the late 1950s and all records were transferred to the Air Force. Therefore the Army isn't aware of what their function was even though it was a Secret unit of the Army.

Feb. 15, 1987: The *San Jose Mercury* states that the Pentagon has a "Black Budget" which has become a "Black Hole" for SECRET Projects spending! It is far bigger than the federal budget for education or transportation or agriculture or the environment. These Projects are classified above Top Secret, therefore very few federal investigators have the security clearances necessary to audit black programs.

June 6, 1988: Letter received from Paul F. Bennewitz describing Project Beta: Alien base located in New Mexico consisting of type "Grey" Aliens. NASA film has aided in locating this base and revealing US Military involvement with the "Greys". Aliens helped US Military to build working saucer, Atomic Powered. Two women and a boy exposed to radiation burns by this saucer. Government is not picking up the medical bills. "Grey" base is currently abandoned. Another group called "Orange" is based on the west slope of Mt. Archeleta near "the Diamond". Goal of Project Beta: to locate, inventory and propose ways of destroying Alien bases!

HOWARD W. CANNON, NEV., CHAIRMAN

WARREN G. MAGNUSON, WASH.	BOB PACKWOOD, OREG.
RUSSELL B. LONG, LA.	BARRY GOLDWATER, ARIZ.
ERNEST F. HOLLINGS, S.C.	HARRISON H. SCHMITT, N. MEX.
ANIEL K. INOUYE, HAWAII	JOHN C. DANFORTH, MO.
ADLAI E. STEVENSON, ILL.	NANCY KASSEBAUM, KANS.
WENDELL H. FORD, KY.	LARRY PRESSLER, S. DAK.
DONALD W. RIEGLE, JR., MICH.	JOHN W. WARNER, VA.
J. JAMES EXON, NEBR.	
HOWELL HEFLIN, ALA.	

AUBREY L. SARVIS, STAFF DIRECTOR AND CHIEF COUNSEL
EDWIN K. HALL, GENERAL COUNSEL
MALCOLM M. B. STERRETT, MINORITY STAFF DIRECTOR

United States Senate

COMMITTEE ON COMMERCE, SCIENCE,
AND TRANSPORTATION

WASHINGTON, D.C. 20510

April 11, 1979

Mr. Lee M. Graham
526 West Maple
Monrovia, California 91016

Dear Mr. Graham:

It is true I was denied access to a facility at Wright-Patterson. Because I never got in, I can't tell you what was inside. We both know about the rumors.

Apart from that, let me make my position clear: I do not believe that we are the only planet, and of some two billion that exist, that has life on it. I have never seen what I would call a UFO, but I have intelligent friends who have, so I can sort of argue either way.

Sincerely,

Barry Goldwater